The
Tower Air Fryer
Cookbook

1001-Day Easy and Affordable Recipes for Your Tower Air Fryer

Toby Vincent

CONTENTS

Introduction
Why We Love Using An Air Fryer

The air fryer is one of the hottest healthy cooking appliances to hit the market in recent years, and for good reason: It can deliver low-fat alternatives to typically deep-fried foods.

The air fryer BENEFITS: It is compact and mobile; It is convenient and easy to cook in; Preheating, if required is of short duration- only a few minutes; The device can be left alone - no constant monitoring required; None or very little splattering; They don't heat up your kitchen - great for summers I'd say; Healthy - none or very little oil used, depends on what you are cooking; Super easy to clean; For picky eaters, air-frying is an excellent method for crisping up vegetables and making them more delightful.

Great- tasting food, didn't I already say that earlier but yes that's one of the biggest reasons why we love ours!

HOW DOES AN AIR FRYER WORK?

Air fryers are used in place of typical roasting, frying, or grilling equipment. They make it possible to get crispy, fried textures without using any oil. An air fryer works much like a convection oven. With convection roasting, warm air is circulated at a high temperature, cooking food from all sides. Unlike an oven, though, its compact size allows it to circulate hot air more quickly around food. In turn, your food cooks about 20 percent faster while achieving a crispier texture.

AIR FRYERS CAN REPLACE OVENS

One of the best features of air fryers is that they can replace many of the functions of your typical oven, not only roasting and broiling but also—with the help of inserts or pans—baking. This makes them incredible for anyone without access to an oven, such as college students living in dorms. As long as you have access to an electrical outlet, you can cook all of your favorite oven-roasted foods in an air fryer.

WHAT CAN YOU COOK IN AN AIR FRYER?

Because an air fryer is primarily used to replace roasting and frying, the best foods are those that you would typically roast or fry. Potatoes are a popular option. You can also air fry Brussels sprouts, corn on the cob, sweet potatoes, onion rings, and even Buffalo Cauliflower Bites. You don't need to add oil when roasting in the air fryer. Simply season the vegetables, set the timer, and let them cook.

You can also use your air fryer for baking. Using inserts or pans, you can bake stuffed apples and stuffed sweet potatoes; you can even bake bread. You can also bake veggie burgers and tofu. The intense heat will mean a quicker cooking time. Plus, you don't have to turn on the oven.

The instruction manual that comes with the appliance will guide you on basic cooking times and temperatures.

DO YOU NEED TO USE OIL IN AN AIR FRYER?

No! The air fryer is perfect for oil-free cooking. Though manufacturers and recipes often suggest using a little bit of oil, you actually don't need to add any oil to ingredients before tossing them into the fryer basket. The high heat and circulating air will give you crispy texture without any oil. Just be sure to remove the basket and shake the contents a couple of times during cooking to prevent sticking.

WHAT SHOULD I AVOID COOKING IN THE AIR FRYER?

Avoid cooking grains, rice, or any food that needs to absorb liquid, and anything small enough to fall through the perforations in the bottom of the cooking basket. Also, be cautious if you're coating ingredients in a wet batter before air frying. You want to ensure the batter isn't runny. Otherwise, it may drip through the bottom of the basket.

Tips For Cooking In An Air Fryer

- Grease your Air-fryer basket---This will prevent food from sticking to the basket
- Avoid overcrowding the basket---If you want your foods to be brown and crisp, place them such that they are not sticking to each other.
- Use a tiny bit of oil---Using a little oil will help the foods to be crispy. If the food has some fat already, then you do not need to use oil.
- Spray oil midway---Spraying with oil halfway through cooking gives you the best crispness on most foods.
- Use optimum temperature---Foods dry quickly in the air fryer. So adjust the temperature accordingly. It'll be lesser than what you would use in the oven.
- Shake the basket during cooking---Shake the basket every few minutes when air frying smaller items like french fries, kale chips, broccoli etc. and similar items to ensure uniform cooking. You can also turn them with tongs.

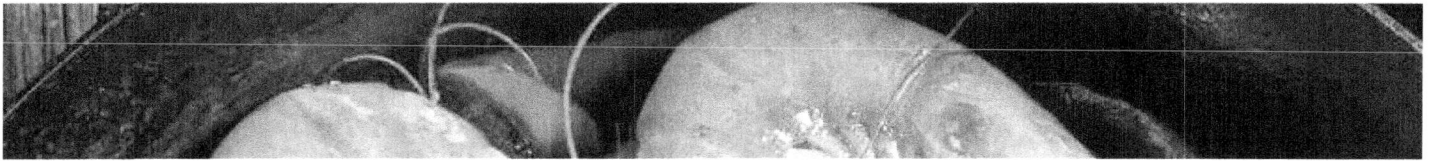

Air Fryer Seafood and Shrimp

Air Fryer Cajun Shrimp Dinner

Ingredients:

- 1 tablespoon Cajun or Creole seasoning
- 24 (1 pound) cleaned and peeled extra jumbo shrimp
- 6 ounces fully cooked Turkey/Chicken Andouille sausage or kielbasa* (sliced)
- 1 medium zucchini (8 ounces, sliced into 1/4-inch thick half moons)
- 1 medium yellow squash (8 ounces, sliced into 1/4-inch thick half moons)
- 1 large red bell pepper (seeded and cut into thin 1-inch pieces)
- 1/4 teaspoon kosher salt
- 2 tablespoons olive oil

Directions:

1. In a large bowl, combine the Cajun seasoning and shrimp, toss to coat.
2. Add the sausage, zucchini, squash, bell peppers, and salt and toss with the oil.
3. Preheat the air fryer 400F.
4. In 2 batches (for smaller baskets), transfer the shrimp and vegetables to the air fryer basket and cook 8 minutes, shaking the basket 2 to 3 times.
5. Set aside, repeat with remaining shrimp and veggies.
6. Once both batches are cooked, return the first batch to the air fryer and cook 1 minute.

Keto Shrimp Scampi

Ingredients:

- 4 tablespoons Butter
- 1 tablespoon Lemon Juice
- 1 tablespoon Minced Garlic
- 2 teaspoons Red Pepper Flakes
- 1 tablespoon chopped chives, or 1 teaspoon dried chives
- 1 tablespoon chopped fresh basil, or 1 teaspoon dried basil
- 2 tablespoons Chicken Stock, (or white wine)
- 1 lb (453.59 g) Raw Shrimp, (21-25 count)

Directions:

1. Turn your air fryer to 330F. Place a 6 x 3 metal pan in it and allow it to start heating while you gather your ingredients.
2. Place the butter, garlic, and red pepper flakes into the hot 6-inch pan.
3. Allow it to cook for 2 minutes, stirring once, until the butter has melted. Do not skip this step. This is what infuses garlic into the butter, which is what makes it all taste so good.
4. Open the air fryer, add butter, lemon juice,, minced garlic, red pepper flakes, chives, basil, chicken stock, and shrimp to the pan in the order listed, stirring gently.
5. Allow shrimp to cook for 5 minutes, stirring once. At this point, the butter should be well-melted and liquid, bathing the shrimp in spiced goodness.
6. Mix very well, remove the 6-inch pan using silicone mitts, and let it rest for 1 minute on the counter. You're doing this so that you let the shrimp cook in the residual heat, rather than letting it accidentally overcook and get rubbery.
7. Stir at the end of the minute. The shrimp should be well-cooked at this point.
8. Sprinkle additional fresh basil leaves and enjoy.

Keto Coconut Shrimp

Ingredients:

- For the shrimp:
- 1 pound shrimp peeled & cleaned
- ¾ Cup all-purpose flour
- 1 teaspoon each onion & garlic powder
- 2 eggs lightly beaten
- ½ Cup each panko breadcrumbs & unsweetened shredded coconut flakes
- Kosher salt & fresh pepper
- Avocado or grapeseed oil
- ½ Cup full fat mayonnaise
- Zest & juice of half a lime

- 1 clove garlic finely grated
- 2-3 tablespoons sriracha or hot sauce
- For the keto coconut shrimp:
- ¾ Cup coconut flour
- 1 teaspoon each onion & garlic powder
- 2 eggs lightly beaten
- ½ Cup each pork rind crumbs & unsweetened shredded coconut flakes
- Kosher salt & fresh pepper
- Avocado or grapeseed oil

Directions:

1. For the keto coconut shrimp, prepare the dredge station by adding the coconut flour, onion & garlic powder, ½ teaspoon salt, and a few cracks of pepper to a shallow dish, mix well. Add the eggs to a small dish/bowl and lightly whisk. Add the pork rinds to a zip-top bag and use a rolling pin to bash them into breadcrumbs the size of panko. Add them to a dish along with the coconut flakes, ¼ teaspoon salt, few cracks of pepper, and mix well.
2. Season the shrimp with a little pinch of salt on bot sides then dredge in the coconut flour shake off any excess, dredge in the eggs, shake off any excess, dredge in the pork rind and coconut flakes and make sure the shrimp is well covered. Move shrimp to a wire rack set over a sheet tray. Repeat the process with the remaining shrimp.
3. For the regular version of the coconut shrimp, follow the same exact steps but you all-purpose flour instead of coconut, and panko breadcrumbs instead of pork rinds.
4. Pour 2 inches of oil into a frying pan and bring the temperature to 340-350 F. While the oil is coming to temperature, it's ok that the shrimp sit at room temperature so the coating ca firm up. Fry the shrimp in batches, for 2-3 minutes on each side, or until golden brown. Remove shrimp and place on a clean wire rack and fry the next batch.
5. Make the sriracha dipping sauce by combining all the ingredients in a small bowl and whisking well. Check for seasoning, you may need more sriracha if you like it spicy.
6. If using an air fryer to make the coconut shrimp, spray the basket with non-stick and fry for 8 minutes at 390 F, flipping the shrimp half way.

Air Fryer Lemon Pepper Shrimp

Servings: 2   **Cook Time: 10 Mins**   **Prep Time: 5 Mins**

Ingredients:

- 1/2 tablespoon olive oil plus extra to spray air fryer basket
- 1 Lemon juiced
- 1 tsp lemon pepper
- ¼ tsp paprika
- ¼ tsp garlic powder
- 12 ounces uncooked medium shrimp peeled and deveined
- 1 lemon sliced optional for garnish

Directions:

1. Preheat an air fryer to 400 degrees F
2. Combine olive oil, lemon juice, lemon pepper, paprika, and garlic powder in a medium bowl.
3. Add shrimp and toss until well coated.
4. Lightly spray air fryer basket with non-aerosol olive oil. Place shrimp in the air fryer basket in a single layer.
5. Air fry until the shrimp are opaque with pink accents and firm, 6 to 8 minutes. Shake the basket halfway through cooking, if desired.
6. For extra flavor you can pour any extra marinade over the shrimp in the air fryer before cooking. This is optional.
7. Serve with lemon slices, if desired.

Garlic Parmesan Air Fried Shrimp Recipe

Servings: 6　　**Cook Time: 10 Mins**　　**Prep Time: 5 Mins**

Ingredients:

- 1lb shrimp, deveined and peeled (you can leave tails on if desired)
- 1 tbsp olive oil
- 1 tsp salt
- 1 tsp fresh cracked pepper
- 1 tbsp lemon juice
- 6 cloves garlic, diced
- 1/2 cup grated parmesan cheese
- 1/4 cup diced cilantro or parsley, to garnish (optional)

Directions:

1. In a large bowl, add shrimp and coat in olive oil and lemon juice, season with salt and pepper, and garlic.
2. Cover with plastic wrap and refrigerate for 1-3 hours. (Optional, for more lemon flavor.)
3. Toss parmesan cheese into bowl with shrimp, creating a "breading" for the shrimp.
4. Preheat air fryer.
5. Set air fryer to 350 for 10 minutes, add shrimp to basket, and cook.
6. Shrimp is done when it is opaque white and pink.
7. Serve immediately.

Air Fryer Parmesan Shrimp

Ingredients:

- 2 pounds jumbo cooked shrimp, peeled and deveined
- 4 cloves garlic, minced
- 2/3 cup parmesan cheese, grated
- 1 teaspoon pepper
- 1/2 teaspoon oregano
- 1 teaspoon basil
- 1 teaspoon onion powder
- 2 tablespoons olive oil
- Lemon, quartered

Directions:

1. In a large bowl, combine garlic, parmesan cheese, pepper, oregano, basil, onion powder and olive oil.
2. Gently toss shrimp in mixture until evenly-coated.
3. Spray air fryer basket with non-stick spray and place shrimp in basket.
4. Cook at 350 degrees for 8-10 minutes or until seasoning on shrimp is browned.
5. Squeeze the lemon over the shrimp before serving.

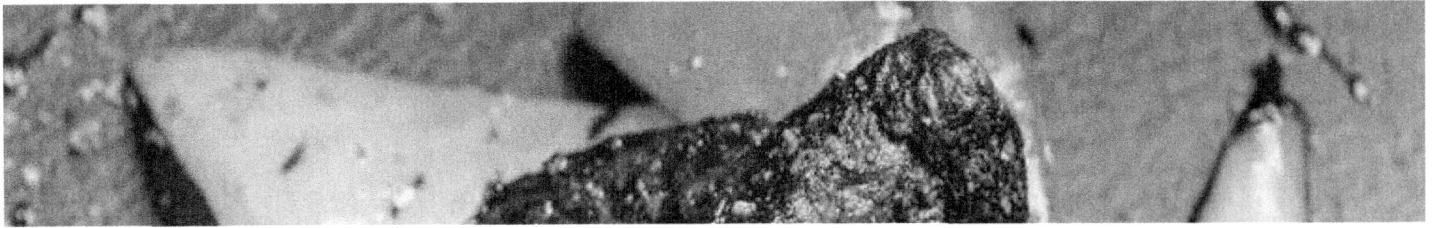

Air Fryer Keto Beef

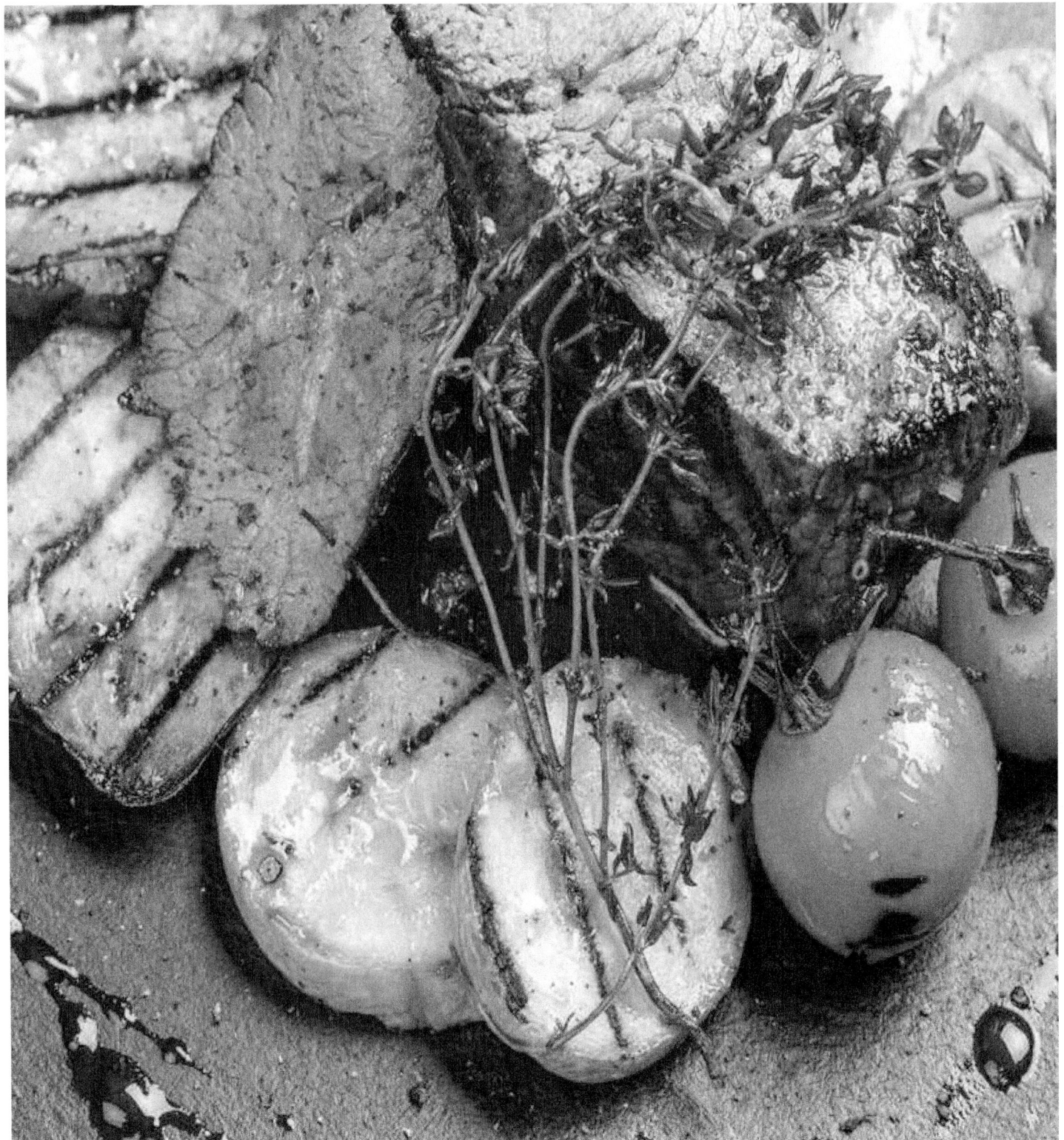

Air Fried Steak And Asparagus Bundles

Ingredients:

- 2 - 2 1/2 pounds Flank steak - cut into 6 pieces
- Kosher salt/black pepper
- 1/2 cup Tamari sauce
- 2 cloves garlic - crushed
- 1 pound asparagus - trimmed
- 3 bell peppers - seeded and sliced thinly
- 1/4 cup balsamic vinegar
- 1/3 cup beef broth
- 2 tablespoons unsalted butter
- Olive oil spray

Directions:

1. Season steaks with salt and pepper.
2. Place steaks into a large zip top bag. Add: Tamari sauce and garlic. Seal bag.
3. Massage steaks so that they're completely coated. Transfer to refrigerator and allow to marinade for a minimum of 1 hour up to overnight.
4. When ready to assemble, remove steaks from marinade and place on a cutting board or sheet. Discard marinade.
5. Equally divide and then place asparagus and bell peppers into the middle of each piece of steak.
6. Roll steak around vegetables and secure with tooth picks.
7. Preheat air fryer.
8. Working in batches, depending on the size of your air fryer, place bundles into basket of air fryer.
9. Spray vegetables with olive oil spray.
10. Cook at 400 degrees for 5 minutes.
11. Remove steak bundles and allow to rest for 5 minutes prior to serving/slicing.
12. WHILE steak is resting, into small-medium sauce pan heat: balsamic vinegar, broth and butter over medium heat. Whisk to combine.
13. Continue cooking until sauce has thickened and reduced by half. Season with salt and pepper.
14. Pour sauce over steak bundles prior to serving.

15

Air Fryer Steak Bites and Mushrooms

Servings: 4   **Cook Time: 20 Mins**   **Prep Time: 10 Mins**

Ingredients:

- 1 lb. (455 g) steaks , cut into 1" cubes & patted dry
- 8 oz. (227 g) mushrooms (cleaned, washed and halved)
- 2 Tablespoons (30 ml) Butter , melted (or oil)
- 1 teaspoon (5 ml) Worcestershire sauce
- 1/2 teaspoon (2.5 ml) garlic powder
- salt , to taste
- Black pepper , to taste
- Minced parsley , garnish
- Melted butter for finishing , optional
- Chili Flakes , for finishing, optional
- Equipment
- Air Fryer

Directions:

1. Combine the steak cubes and mushrooms. Coat with the melted butter and then season with Worcestershire sauce, garlic powder, salt and pepper.
2. Preheat the Air Fryer at 400°F for 4 minutes.
3. Spread the steak and mushrooms in even layer in air fryer basket. Air fry at 400°F for 10-18 minutes, shaking and flipping and the steak and mushrooms about 3 times through cooking process (time depends on your preferred doneness, thickness of the steak, size of the air fryer).
4. Check the steak to see how well done it is cooked. If you want the steak more done, add an extra 2-5 minutes of cooking time.
5. Garnish with parsley and drizzle with optional melted butter and/or optional chili flakes. Season with additional salt & pepper if desired. Serve warm.

Air Fryer Meatballs

Servings: 4   **Cook Time: 15 Mins**   **Prep Time: 10 Mins**

Ingredients:

- 1 pound Lean Ground Beef
- 1/4 cup onions, chopped
- 1/4 cup Cilantro chopped
- 1 tablespoon Minced Garlic
- 2 tablespoons Taco Seasoning
- 1/2 cup Mexican Blend Shredded Cheese
- 1 Eggs
- Kosher Salt
- Ground Black Pepper

FOR DIPPING SAUCE

- 1/4 cup sour cream
- 1/2 cup salsa
- 1-2 Cholula hot sauce

Directions:

1. Place all ingredients in a stand mixer bowl. Using the paddle attachment, beat the mix together until it forms a sticky paste, about 2-3 minutes.
2. Form into 12 meatballs. Place meatballs in the air fryer basket. Set the airfryer to 400F for 10 minutes.
3. Meanwhile mix together the sauce: in a small bowl, mix together the sour cream, salsa, and hot sauce. Serve with the meatballs.

Air Fryer Steak Tips

| |

Ingredients:

- 1.5 lb steak (Ribeye, New York) or beef chuck for a cheaper version cut to 3/4 inch cubes
- Air Fryer Steak Marinade
- 1 tsp oil
- 1/4 tsp salt
- 1/2 tsp black pepper, freshly ground
- 1/2 tsp dried garlic powder
- 1/2 tsp dried onion powder
- 1 tsp Montreal Steak Seasoning
- 1/8 tsp cayenne pepper
- Air Fryer Asparagus
- 1 lb Asparagus, tough ends trimmed (could replace with spears of zucchini)
- 1/4 tsp salt
- 1/2 tsp oil (optional)

Directions:

1. Preheat the air fryer at 400F for about 5 minutes.
2. Meanwhile, trim the steak of any fat and cut it into cubes. Then, toss with the ingredients for the marinade (oil, salt, black pepper, Montreal seasoning, onion and garlic powder & the cayenne pepper) and massage the spices into the meat to coat evenly. Do this in a ziplock bag for easier cleanup.
3. Spray the bottom of the air fryer basket with nonstick spray if you have any and spread the prepared meat along the bottom of it. Cook the beef steak tips for about 4-6 minutes and check for doneness.
4. Toss the asparagus with 1/2 tsp oil and 1/4 tsp salt until evenly coated.
5. Once the steak bites are browned to your liking, toss them around and move to one side. Add the asparagus to the other side of the air fryer basket and cook for another 3 minutes.
6. Remove the steak tips and the asparagus to a serving plate and serve while hot.

Perfect Air Fryer Steak

Servings: 2   **Cook Time: 12 Mins**   **Prep Time: 20 Mins**

Ingredients:

- 2 8 oz Ribeye steak
- salt
- freshly cracked black pepper
- olive oil*
- Garlic Butter
- 1 stick unsalted butter softened
- 2 Tablespoon fresh parsley chopped
- 2 teaspoon garlic minced
- 1 teaspoon Worcestershire Sauce
- 1/2 teaspoon salt

Directions:

Garlic Butter

1. Prepare Garlic Butter by mixing butter, parsley garlic, worcestershire sauce, and salt until thoroughly combined.
2. Place in parchment paper and roll into a log. Refrigerate until ready to use.
3. Air Fryer Steak
4. Remove steak from fridge and allow to sit at room temperature for 20 minutes. Rub a little bit of olive oil on both side of the steak and season with salt and freshly cracked black pepper.
5. Grease your Air Fryer basket by rubbing a little bit of oil on the basket. Preheat Air Fryer to 400 degrees Fahrenheit. Once preheated, place steaks in air fryer and cook for 12 minutes, flipping halfway through.*
6. Remove from air fryer and allow to rest for 5 minutes. Top with garlic butter.

Juicy Air Fryer Steak

Servings: 2   **Cook Time: 10 Mins**   **Prep Time: 5 Mins**

Ingredients:

- 2 New York Strip Steaks Mine were about 6-8 oz each. You can use any type of steak.
- 1 tablespoon low-sodium soy sauce This is used to provide liquid to marinate the meat and make it juicy.
- 1 teaspoon liquid smoke
- melted butter (optional)
- Homemade Steak Rub (Feel free to use a store-bought rub if you wish)
- 1/2 tablespoon unsweetened cocoa powder
- 1 teaspoon brown sugar or sweetener
- 1 teaspoon smoked paprika
- 1/2 teaspoon onion powder
- 1/2 teaspoon garlic powder
- 1/2 teaspoon chili powder
- salt and pepper to taste

Directions:

1. Drizzle the steak with soy sauce and liquid smoke.
2. Season the steak with the spices. Rub the spices into the steak. If you wish to marinate, place the steaks in the fridge for an hour to overnight. This is optional.
3. Place the steak in the air fryer. Do not stack. Cook in batches if necessary.
4. Cook for 5 minutes on 370 degrees. After 5 minutes, open the air fryer and examine your steak. Cook time will vary depending on your desired doneness. Use a meat thermometer and cook to 125° F for rare, 135° F for medium-rare, 145° F for medium, 155° F for medium-well, and 160° F for well done.
5. Mine took 7-8 minutes total for medium doneness.
6. Remove the steak from the air fryer and drizzle with optional melted butter.
7. Allow the steak to rest for at least 3 minutes before slicing or consuming. If you slice into the steak too soon, that will cause that the inside moisture within the steak to spill out onto the plate, leaving a drier, less flavorful steak.

Keto Steak Nuggets

Servings: 4 **Cook Time: X Mins** **Prep Time: X Mins**

Ingredients:

- 1 pound venison steak or beef steak, cut into chunks.
- 1 large Egg(s)
- Lard or palm oil for frying
- Keto Breading
- 1/2 cup grated parmesan cheese
- 1/2 cup pork panko
- 1/2 teaspoon Homemade Seasoned Salt
- Chipotle Ranch Dip
- 1/4 cup mayonnaise
- 1/4 cup Sour Cream
- 1+ teaspoon chipotle paste to taste
- 1/2 teaspoon Homemade Ranch Dressing & Dip Mix
- 1/4 medium lime, juiced

Directions:

1. For the Chipotle Ranch Dip: Combine all ingredients, mix well. 1 teaspoon of chipotle paste yields a medium-spice version, use more or less according to your own taste preferences. I encourage you to use my homemade ranch dressing and dip mix, it's superior to any store brought version. Refrigerate at least 30 minutes before serving, will keep for up to 1 week.
2. Combine Pork Panko, parmesan cheese and seasoned salt - again use my homemade not the store bought stuff. Set aside.
3. Beat 1 egg.. place beaten egg 1 bowl and breading mix in another.
4. Dip chunks of steak in egg, then breading. Place on a wax paper lined sheet pan or plate.
5. FREEZE breaded raw steak bites for 30 minutes before frying. This helps to ensure that the breading will NOT LIFT when fried.
6. Heat Lard to roughly 325 degrees F. Working in batches as necessary, fry steak nuggets (from frozen or chilled) until browned, about 2-3 minutes.
7. Transfer to a papertowel lined plate, season with a sprinkle of salt and serve with Chipotle Ranch.

Air Fryer Beef Kabobs

Servings: 4 **Cook Time: 10 Mins** **Prep Time: 30 Mins**

Ingredients:

- 1 lb beef chuck ribs cut in 1 inch pieces or any other tender cut meat- think nice steak, stew meat
- 1/3 cup low fat sour cream
- 2 tbsp soy sauce
- 1 bell peppers
- 1/2 onion
- 8 6 inch skewers

Directions:

1. Mix sour cream with soy sauce in a medium bowl. Place beef chunks into the bowl and marinate for at least 30 minutes, better overnight
2. Cut bell pepper and onion in 1 inch pieces. Soak wooden skewers in water for about 10 minutes
3. Thread beef, onions and bell peppers onto skewers. Add some freshly ground black pepper.
4. Cook in preheated to 400F Air fryer for 10 minutes, turning half way.

Air Fryer Steak

Servings: 1 **Cook Time: 8 Mins** **Prep Time: 5 Mins**

Ingredients:

- Sirloin steak (or your favourite cut of steak)
- Oil (optional)
- Seasoning

Directions:

1. Take the steak out of the fridge and leave it out for at least 30 minutes so that it can get to room temperature.
2. Preheat the air fryer to 200C.
3. Optionally rub some oil on both sides of the steak and season according to taste.
4. Place in the air fryer - either on a trivet or directly on the base of the air fryer basket.
5. Set the air fryer timer to your desired time, depending on how well you want it cooked.
6. Turn the steak over half way through.
7. At the end of the cooking time check the steak is cooked to your liking and remove it from the air fryer and leave it to rest for at least 5 minutes.

Keto Air Fryer Double Cheeseburger

Ingredients:

- 1/2 lb ground beef (or two pre-made beef patties)
- 2 slices cheese of choice
- 1 pinch pink Himalayan salt
- 1 pinch fresh ground black pepper
- 1 pinch onion powder

Directions:

1. Form two 1/4 pound hamburger patties (if not using pre-made ones)
2. Lightly salt, pepper, and onion powder the hamburger patties
3. Place into your air fryer and set to 370°F for 12 minutes
4. At the 6 minute mark, flip the hamburgers
5. When the air fryer finishes, place the cheese onto the hamburger patties and shut the drawer for one minute
6. Remove the patties, stack, and devour!

Air Fryer Side Dishes

Air Fryer Roasted Cauliflower

Ingredients:

- 4 cups chopped cauliflower
- 1 Tbs olive oil
- 1 tsp parsley
- 1 tsp thyme
- 1 tsp minced garlic
- 1 tsp salt
- ¼ Cup parmesan cheese
- Salt and pepper to taste

Directions:

1. In a large bowl combine cauliflower with olive oil parsley, thyme, minced garlic, and salt.
2. Toss to combine and cauliflower is well coated.
3. Place cauliflower in air-fryer basket. Set air-fryer to 400 degrees for 20 minutes.
4. Stir the cauliflower at 10 minutes, and add parmesan cheese.
5. Serve immediately, season with salt and pepper to taste.

Pizza Rolls

Ingredients:

- 240g natural/Greek yoghurt
- 350g self raising flour
- 1 tin/carton of passata/pizza sauce (or enough to cover the dough)
- Grated cheese (your favourite, I like to use Mozzarella)
- 1tsp dried herbs (optional)

Directions:

1. In a bowl, mix together the flour and yoghurt until a dough is formed. If the mixture is too wet and sticky, add in some more flour. If it is too dry, add in a little water. You need to be able to roll out the dough without it sticking or falling about.
2. On a lightly floured work surface roll out the dough into a rectangle.
3. Spread the pizza sauce/passata across the dough. You can use your favourite pizza sauce, or just some regular pasta sauce. Be careful it isn't too runny though or it will just run off the dough. I like to use the Pizza Express pizza sauce cans you can get.
4. Sprinkle your grated cheese over the tomato sauce and add your favourite toppings.
5. Carefully roll the pizza over lengthwise until it is in a sausage shape.
6. Using a sharp knife, or a serrated knife, slice the pizza roll up into even slices.
7. Carefully place the pizza rolls on either a baking tray (if cooking in an oven) or directly to your air fryer basket.
8. Cook at 180C for about 8 minutes, or 12 minutes in an oven. Check on them half way through to make sure they are not cooking too quickly.

Breakfast Frittata

Ingredients:

- Oil or butter to grease the pan
- 3 eggs
- 1/4 red pepper, diced
- 1/4 green pepper, diced
- 10 baby spinach leaves, chopped
- Handful of cheddar cheese, grated
- Salt and pepper to season, optional

Directions:

1. In a bowl beat the eggs. Season with salt and pepper if required.
2. Grease the pan with the oil or butter and place it in the air fryer. Switch to 180C/350F and allow to heat for a minute. Add the peppers and cook for 3 minutes.
3. Pour the spinach and egg mix in. Sprinkle the grated cheese across the top. Cook for a further 6 minutes, checking half way through to make sure it isn't over cooking.

Notes

You Will Also Need:Pizza base/quiche/flan tin

Air Fryer Chickpeas

Ingredients:

- 1 x 400g tin chickpeas, drained and rinsed
- 1 tbsp olive oil
- 2 tsp spice or herb seasoning*

Directions:

1. Drain and rinse the chickpeas.
2. Add the oil and your choice of spices or herbs (see notes).
3. Toss the chickpeas until they are coated in the oil and seasoning.
4. Transfer to the air fryer basket and set off at 200°C (190°F), and air fry for 15 minutes, shaking two or three times.
5. The chickpeas should be hard and crispy when they are ready. If they are still a little soft, air fry them for a few more minutes. Add extra seasoning if required.

Notes

*Seasoning

You can use any seasoning you like. Suggestions include;

Piri Piri

Smoked Paprika

Garlic Salt

Garlic and Herb

Mixed Herbs

Curry Powder

Air Fryer Banana Bread

Ingredients:

- 2 ripe bananas, medium in size
- 120g butter, softened
- 100g caster sugar
- 200g self-raising flour
- 2 medium eggs, beaten
- 1tsp baking powder
- 1tsp ground cinnamon

Directions:

1. Mix together the butter and sugar until they are smooth. Then slowly add the beaten eggs and mix until they are combined.
2. Add the flour, baking powder and ground cinnamon, followed by the mashed bananas.
3. Stir everything together gently until combined.
4. Transfer the mixture to a greased baking tin and place it in the air fryer at 160°C. Set the timer for 30 minutes.
5. At the end of the cooking time, the banana bread should be browned on the outside and cooked all the way through. Insert a metal skewer to check it isn't wet or soggy on the inside. If it needs to be cooked for longer, check on it every 5 minutes to ensure it doesn't burn. If the outside is already browned, you might need to cover it in some foil.

Air fryer Brussels sprouts recipe

Ingredients:

- 2 cups Brussels sprouts sliced lengthwise into ¼" thick pieces (see notes)
- 1 tablespoon olive oil OR maple syrup See note.
- 1 tablespoon balsamic vinegar
- 1/4 teaspoon sea salt

Directions:

1. In a bowl, toss together the Brussels, oil or maple syrup, vinegar, and salt.
2. Cook at 400F for 8-10 minutes, shaking (and checking their progress) after 5 minutes and then at 8 the minute mark. You're going for crispy and browned, but not burnt!

Notes

I can't stress enough how important it is to get ¼" thick pieces. Thicker slices will not cook fully. Slice the sprouts lengthwise. Depending on the size of your Brussels sprouts, that might mean cutting them in half, thirds, or more.

If you prefer softer Brussels sprouts, soak the slices in water for 10 minutes. Then, drain them, pat them dry, season them, and proceed with the recipe.

Use maple syrup for an oil free option. Just note that if you ditch the oil, the finished product won't be quite as crispy as the version with oil. But it's still delicious!

Calorie count is for the recipe with oil, because it's my favorite way to make these!

Leftovers will keep in an airtight container in the refrigerator for 3-4 days. You can serve leftovers warm or cold.

To reheat, either pop them into the microwave or the air fryer. In the air fryer, reheat these at 350° F for 5-7 minutes.

Air Fryer Roasted Asian Broccoli

Ingredients:

- 1 Lb Broccoli, Cut into florets
- 1 1/2 Tbsp Peanut oil
- 1 Tbsp Garlic, minced
- Salt
- 2 Tbsp Reduced sodium soy sauce
- 2 tsp Honey (or agave)
- 2 tsp Sriracha
- 1 tsp Rice vinegar
- 1/3 Cup Roasted salted peanuts
- Fresh lime juice (optional)

Directions:

1. In a large bowl, toss together the broccoli, peanut oil, garlic and season with sea salt. Make sure the oil covers all the broccoli florets. I like to use my hands to give each one a quick rub.
2. Spread the broccoli into the wire basket of your air fryer, in as single of a layer, as possible, trying to leave a little bit of space between each floret.
3. Cook at 400 degrees until golden brown and crispy, about 15 – 20 minutes, stirring halfway.
4. While the broccoli cook, mix together the honey, soy sauce, sriracha and rice vinegar in a small, microwave-safe bowl.
5. Once mixed, microwave the mixture for 10-15 seconds until the honey is melted, and evenly incorporated.
6. Transfer the cooked broccoli to a bowl and add in the soy sauce mixture. Toss to coat and season to taste with a pinch more salt, if needed.
7. Stir in the peanuts and squeeze lime on top (if desired.)
8. DEVOUR!

TIPS & NOTES:

You can also roast this in a 425 degree oven on a large pan, making sure to not crowd the broccoli. Cook for about 20 minutes, stirring halfway. You will also need 2 Tbsp of Peanut oil.

Air Fryer Apricot and Raisin Cake

Servings: 8   **Cook Time: 12 Mins**   **Prep Time: 10 Mins**

Ingredients:

- 75g dried apricots, (just under 1/2 cup)
- 4 tbsp orange juice
- 75g self-raising flour, (3/4 cup)
- 40 g Sugar, (1/3 cup)
- 1 egg
- 75g Raisins, (just under 1/2 a cup)

Directions:

1. Preheat air fryer to 160C/320F
2. In a blender or food processor blend the dried apricots and juice until they are smooth.
3. In a separate bowl, mix together the sugar and flour.
4. Beat the egg. Add it to the flour and sugar. Mix together.
5. Add the apricot puree and raisins. Combine together.
6. Spray an air fryer safe baking tin with a little oil. Transfer the mixture over and level off.
7. Cook in the air fryer for 12 minutes, check it at 10 minutes. Use a metal skewer to see if it is done. If need be, return the cake to the air fryer to cook for a few more minutes to brown up.
8. Allow to cool before removing from the baking tin and slicing up.

Air Fryer Carrot Cake

Servings: X   **Cook Time: 25 Mins**   **Prep Time: 10 Mins**

Ingredients:

- 140g Soft brown sugar
- 2 eggs, beaten
- 140g butter
- 1 orange, zest & juice
- 200g self-raising flour
- 1tsp ground cinnamon
- 175g grated carrot, (approx 2 medium carrots)
- 60g sultanas

Directions:

1. Preheat air fryer to 175C.
2. In a bowl, cream together the butter and sugar.
3. Slowly add the beaten eggs.
4. Fold in the flour, a little bit at a time, mixing it as you go. Add the orange juice and zest, grated carrots and sultanas. Gently mix all the ingredients together.
5. Grease the baking tin and pour the mixture in.
6. Place baking tin in the air fryer basket and cook for 25-30 minutes. Check and see if the cake has cooked - use a cocktail stick or metal skewer to poke in the middle. If it comes out wet then cook it for a little longer.
7. Remove the baking tin from the air fryer basket and allow to cool for 10 minutes before removing from the tin.

Air Fryer Sausages

Servings: 8 **Cook Time: 10 Mins** **Prep Time: 3 Mins**

Ingredients:

- 8 sausages

Directions:

1. Preheat the air fryer to 180C (350F)
2. Pierce each sausage with a knife or fork.
3. Lay sausages in the air fryer basket.
4. Cook for 10 minutes, checking on them and turning them over after 5 minutes.

Notes

Use any sausages you want to - any flavour and any size. For smaller sausages check on them before 10 minutes as they will cook in a quicker time.

Air Fryer Jacket Potato

Servings: 1 **Cook Time: 40 Mins** **Prep Time: 5 Mins**

Ingredients:

- Baking potato (Maris Piper is a good choice)
- Oil and seasoning

Directions:

1. Scrub and wash each baking potato and pat dry with some kitchen roll. Pierce with a fork and add a little oil on the skin, rubbing it all over. Season with salt if required.
2. Place in the air fryer basket and cook at 200C/400F for 40 minutes. Check on it half way through and turn the potato over. If the potato skin is crisping up too quickly wrap it in some foil.
3. Check the potato is cooked through by piercing it with a fork - it should be soft on the inside.
4. When the potato is ready, slice it in half and top with your favourite jacket potato fillings.

Air Fryer Bacon

Servings: 4   **Cook Time: 10 Mins**   **Prep Time: X Mins**

Ingredients:

- 4 bacon rashers*

Directions:

1. Lay the bacon rashers in the air fryer basket. If you want to fit more rashers in, either use a trivet or a rack to add more. It doesn't matter if the bacon rashers are touching each other, or if they are overlapping a little bit, but don't lay them on top of each other.
2. Set the air fryer off at 180C/350F for 8 to 10 minutes. For thicker slices of bacon increase the time to 12-15 minutes. Flip the bacon half way through (unless you are using a crisping rack).
3. If the bacon isn't crispy enough, cook it for a little longer, checking on it after 2 minutes.

Notes

*you can cook less or more bacon if you wish, the cooking time will be the same.

Simply The Best Air Fryer Roast Potatoes

Servings: 4   **Cook Time: 25 Mins**   **Prep Time: X Mins**

Ingredients:

- 8 medium potatoes (Maris Piper)
- 1 tbsp olive oil

Directions:

1. Preheat airfryer to 180C/350F.
2. Peel and chop up potatoes. The smaller you cut them up the quicker they will cook.
3. Spray/brush with 1tbsp of oil - make sure they are all coated.
4. Put potatoes in air fryer basket and slide into the air fryer.
5. Cook for 25 minutes. Check on them at regular intervals and give them a good shake about.

Crispy Air Fryer Brussels Sprouts

Ingredients:

- 2 cups Brussel sprouts
- 2 Tablespoons coconut oil
- 1/4 cup parmesan cheese grated
- 1/4 cup almonds sliced and crushed
- 2 Tablespoons everything bagel seasoning
- Sea salt to taste

Directions:

1. Add Brussel sprouts to a medium saucepan with 2 cups of water, cover and cook over medium heat for 8-10 minutes.
2. Drain Brussels sprouts and allow to cool, then slice each one in half.
3. Toss Brussel sprouts in a large mixing bowl with oil, parmesan cheese, crushed almonds, everything bagel seasoning, and salt.
4. If needed, use a wooden spoon to stir and make sure the Brussel sprouts are fully coated in seasoning.
5. Transfer the Brussels sprouts to the air fryer, and cook for 12 to 15 minutes at 375 or until golden for both sides.

Air Fryer French Toast

Ingredients:

- 4 slices medium thickness bread
- 2 eggs
- 80ml milk
- 40ml double cream (optinal)
- 1 tsp cinnamon
- 1 tsp vanilla extract
- Optional toppings (berries, icing sugar, maple syrup)

Directions:

1. Slice the bread into halves, quarters or lengthwise into 'soldiers' and lay flat in a shallow dish (you may need to do this in batches).
2. Whisk the eggs with the milk, cream (if using), cinnamon and vanilla extract.
3. Pour the egg mixture over the bread and leave to soak for a few minutes, turning it over halfway.
4. While the bread is soaking, preheat the air fryer to 180°C/350°F
5. Carefully transfer the soaked bread to the air fryer basket and air fry for 8 to 10 minutes, turning halfway.
6. If at the end of the air frying time the bread is not crisp enough, turn the temperature up to 200°C/400°F and air fry for a further 1 minute on each side.
7. Serve as it is or with some fresh berries, bananas, maple syrup or a sprinkling of icing sugar.

Air Fryer Roasted Asian Broccoli

Servings: 4   **Cook Time: 20 Mins**   **Prep Time: 10 Mins**

Ingredients:

- 1 Lb Broccoli, Cut into florets
- 1 1/2 Tbsp Peanut oil
- 1 Tbsp Garlic, minced
- Salt
- 2 Tbsp Reduced sodium soy sauce
- 2 tsp Honey (or agave)
- 2 tsp Sriracha
- 1 tsp Rice vinegar
- 1/3 Cup Roasted salted peanuts
- Fresh lime juice (optional)

Directions:

1. In a large bowl, toss together the broccoli, peanut oil, garlic and season with sea salt. Make sure the oil covers all the broccoli florets. I like to use my hands to give each one a quick rub.
2. Spread the broccoli into the wire basket of your air fryer, in as single of a layer, as possible, trying to leave a little bit of space between each floret.
3. Cook at 400 degrees until golden brown and crispy, about 15 – 20 minutes, stirring halfway.
4. While the broccoli cook, mix together the honey, soy sauce, sriracha and rice vinegar in a small, microwave-safe bowl.
5. Once mixed, microwave the mixture for 10-15 seconds until the honey is melted, and evenly incorporated.
6. Transfer the cooked broccoli to a bowl and add in the soy sauce mixture. Toss to coat and season to taste with a pinch more salt, if needed.
7. Stir in the peanuts and squeeze lime on top (if desired.)
8. Devour!

Air-Fried Asparagus

Servings: 4   **Cook Time: 10 Mins**   **Prep Time: 5 Mins**

Ingredients:

- 1/2 bunch of asparagus, with bottom 2 inches trimmed off
- Avocado or Olive Oil in an oil mister or sprayer
- Himalayan salt
- Black pepper

Directions:

1. Place trimmed asparagus spears in the air-fryer basket. Spritz spears lightly with oil, then sprinkle with salt and a tiny bit of black pepper.
2. Place basket inside air-fryer and bake at 400° for 10 minutes.
3. Serve immediately.

Air Fryer Keto Garlic Cheese 'Bread'

Servings: X   **Cook Time: 10 Mins**   **Prep Time: 5 Mins**

Ingredients:

- 1 cup shredded mozzarella cheese
- ¼ cup grated Parmesan cheese
- 1 large egg
- ½ Teaspoon garlic powder

Directions:

1. Line the air fryer basket with a piece of parchment paper.
2. Combine mozzarella cheese, Parmesan cheese, egg, and garlic powder in a bowl; mix until well combined. Press into a round circle on the parchment in the air fryer basket.
3. Heat the air fryer to 350 degrees F (175 degrees C). Fry bread for 10 minutes. Remove. Serve garlic cheese bread warm, but not hot.

Air Fryer Broccoli

Servings: 4   **Cook Time: 12 Mins**   **Prep Time: 1 Mins**

Ingredients:

- 12 oz Frozen Broccoli Florets
- 2 tablespoon oil We use melted bacon fat or lard
- 1/2 teaspoon garlic powder
- 1/2 teaspoon onion powder
- Salt and pepper to taste

Directions:

1. Toss frozen florets in oil in a bowl.
2. Season with remaining ingredients, tossing to coat.
3. Place in fryer basket and roast at 350 for 10-12 minutes.
4. Serve as is, topped with shredded parm or loaded.

Easy Air Fryer Green Beans

Servings: 4   **Cook Time: 6 Mins**   **Prep Time: 2 Mins**

Ingredients:

- 1 pound (450g) green beans
- Cooking spray
- Salt to taste

Directions:

1. Preheat the air fryer to 400 degrees F / 200 degrees C.
2. Add the green beans to a bowl and spray with some low-calorie spray and the best salt ever and combine.
3. Place the beans into the air fryer basket and cook for 6-8 minutes, turning a couple of times during cooking so that they brown evenly.
4. Remove and serve topped with some extra salt and chopped herbs if you like.

Keto Air Fryer Zucchini Noodles Recipe

Ingredients:

- 4 cups zucchini noodles
- 2 tablespoons mayonnaise
- 1/2 cup parmesan cheese, grated
- Season with salt and black pepper (optional)

Directions:

1. Preheat the air fryer for a few minutes while you make the zucchini noodles.
2. Mix the zucchini noodles, mayo and parmesan cheese in a large bowl. Make sure to coat the noodles well with the mayo then add in the parmesan cheese.
3. Spray the air fryer basket with cooking spray.
4. Place the noodles in the basket and cook at 400°F for 8-10 minutes. Check after 5 minutes to make sure they don't get too brown. If your noodles are thicker it may take longer.

Air Fryer Sweet Potato Wedges

Ingredients:

- 4 large sweet potatoes*
- 1 tbsp oil (I used olive oil)
- 1 tsp smoked paprika
- 1 tsp garlic powder
- Salt and pepper according to taste

Directions:

1. Preheat the air fryer to 200C/190F.
2. Prepare the sweet potatoes by chopping off the ends and cleaning them. Slice them lengthwise into similar-sized wedges.
3. Drizzle with oil and add seasoning. Toss the sweet potato wedges in the oil and seasoning, ensuring they are all coated.
4. Transfer to the air fryer basket and set the timer for 20 minutes. Check on them at the halfway mark to shake them about.
5. After 20 minutes, they should be crispy on the outside and soft and fluffy on the inside. If they are not, return them to the air fryer and continue cooking, checking on them after 2 minutes.
6. Serve the sweet potato wedges as a side dish or with your favourite dip.

Notes

*Sweet Potatoes: if you don't have large sweet potatoes use 2 or 3 mediums ones.

Air Fryer Sweet Potato Fries

Servings: 2   **Cook Time: 12 Mins**   **Prep Time: 5 Mins**

Ingredients:

- 1 large sweet potato, approx 350g, (makes 2 small portions, double up for more)
- 1 tbsp rapeseed oil (other oil of your choice, olive, coconut, avocado etc)
- 2 tsp spice/seasoning mix (ideas include paprika, cayenne, garlic, pepper)
- Salt for seasoning once cooked (optional)

Directions:

1. Preheat the air fryer to 180C (360F) (200C/400F for an oven)
2. Peel the sweet potato (optional).
3. Slice into thin chips.
4. Drizzle with oil, trying to cover as many of the fries as possible.
5. Sprinkle the spice mix over the fries and toss to coat.
6. Lay prepared fries in the air fryer basket (or on parchment paper on a baking tray if using an oven)
7. Cook for 12 minutes, (15 to 20 minutes in an oven), checking halfway to shake about/turn over.

Notes

Remember different air fryer models can cook at different speeds. Until you are familiar with your air fryer, make sure you check on the food frequently to make sure it isn't over cooking.

If the fries aren't crisping up, try to spread them out a bit so that they are not over lapping each other. You can also spray with a little more oil.

Air Fryer Personal Pizza

Ingredients:

- 1 (16-oz) package fresh pizza dough
- 4 tsp olive oil
- 1 cup pizza sauce
- 4 cups shredded mozzarella cheese
- favorite pizza toppings

Directions:

1. Cut dough into 4-equal pieces. Roll and stretch one piece of the pizza dough into a 6-inch round. Lay the dough round in the air fryer, and brush with 1 teaspoon of olive oil.
2. Spread 1/4 cup of pizza sauce on top of dough. Sprinkle 1 cup of mozzarella cheese on top of sauce. Arrange toppings over cheese.
3. Cook at 350°F for 8 minutes.
4. Transfer pizza to a plate and serve immediately.
5. Repeat with remaining dough pieces.

Air Fryer Potato Wedges

| Servings: 4 | Cook Time: 20 Mins | Prep Time: 5 Mins |

Ingredients:

- 4 large potatoes
- 1 to 2 tbsps oil
- 1 tsp seasoning

Directions:

1. Wash and scrub each potato before cutting it into wedges.
2. Either soak the cut potatoes in cold water for up to 30 minutes or rinse them under cold water. Pat the wedges dry with some kitchen roll or a clean tea towel.
3. Brush the wedges with some oil until they are all coated. This step is optional if you would prefer to make oil-free wedges.
4. Season according to your tastes - just a little salt, or you can add some smoked paprika, cayenne pepper, or a little curry powder to make curried potato wedges.
5. Place potato wedges in the air fryer basket - depending on the size of your air fryer, you may need to do this in batches.
6. Cook at 200C/400F for 20 minutes, shaking every 5 minutes.
7. Cook until the wedges are crispy on the outside. The cooking time may be longer if you cook a lot of wedges at the same time.
8. Remove wedges from the air fryer basket and add some more seasoning if required.

Notes

Maris Pipers are a good choice for potato wedges.

Air Fryer Crispy Brussels Sprouts

Ingredients:

- 1 pound Brussels sprouts, stems removed and quartered
- 2 tablespoons oil
- Kosher salt and pepper to taste

Directions:

1. In a large bowl, toss the Brussels sprouts with the oil and salt and pepper. Pour into the Air Fryer basket and lay in a single layer.
2. Cook in the Air Fryer at 350F for 7 minutes. Check to see if the sprouts are tender by piercing with a fork. If not tender, cook at 350F for 3 minutes more.
3. If the sprouts are tender, but not yet crunchy enough, turn the Air fryer up to 375F and cook for 3 minutes. Check for crunchiness and cook longer, if desired.
4. Season to taste.

Air Fryer Garlic And Herb Potatoes

Servings: 4   **Cook Time: 20 Mins**   **Prep Time: 5 Mins**

Ingredients:

- 1kg new potatoes
- 2-3 sprigs rosemary
- Handful fresh parsley
- 2 tbsp garlic granules/powder
- 2 tsp salt
- 2 tbsp of olive oil

Directions:

1. Chop the potatoes into even-sized chunks, halving the medium ones and quartering the large ones.
2. Finely chop the parsley and the rosemary (leaves only).
3. Place the potatoes in a large bowl, and sprinkle over the chopped herbs, the garlic granules and salt. Drizzle over with olive oil and mix until all potatoes are well-coated.
4. Cook in air fryer at 200°C for 20 minutes, shaking after 10 minutes. If you have a smaller air fryer, you may have to cook for longer or in 2 small batches.

Notes

While fresh garlic can be used, garlic granules make it much easier to ensure every potato is evenly garlicky.

Air Fryer Biscuits

Ingredients:

- 1 cup almond flour
- 1/2 tsp baking powder
- 1/4 tsp pink himalayan salt
- 1 cup shredded cheddar cheese
- 2 large eggs
- 2 tbsp butter, melted
- 2 tbsp sour cream

Directions:

1. Combine the almond flour, baking powder, and salt in a large bowl. Mix in the cheddar cheese by hand until well combined.
2. Add eggs, butter, and sour cream to the center and blend with a large fork, spoon, or your hands, until a sticky batter forms.
3. Fit a piece of parchment paper into your air fryer basket. Drop ¼ cup-sized (for large) or 2 tablespoon-sized (for small) portions of batter onto the parchment.
4. Air Fry/"Bake" at 400 degrees F for 6 minutes (for small) to 10 minutes (for large), until golden brown and cooked through. Repeat with remaining batter as needed. Serve immediately!

Note: recipe can yield 9 small biscuits or 5 large biscuits. Nutrition is for 9 small biscuits.

Alternatively, you could place the batter in silicone muffin liners and air fry them for taller biscuits (yields 7-9, bakes 10-12 minutes depending on how much you fill them).

Air Fried Cauliflower Rice

Servings: 3   **Cook Time: X Mins**   **Prep Time: X Mins**

Ingredients:

- Round 1
- 1/2 block firm or extra firm tofu
- 2 tablespoons reduced sodium soy sauce
- 1/2 cup diced onion
- 1 cup diced carrot about 1 ½ to 2 carrots
- 1 teaspoon turmeric
- Round 2
- 3 cups riced cauliflower Cauliflower minced into pieces smaller than the size of a pea. You can do this by hand with a box-style cheese crater, use your food processor to pulse into pieces, or buy pre-riced, bagged cauliflower.
- 2 tablespoons reduced sodium soy sauce
- 1 1/2 teaspoons toasted sesame oil optional, but recommended
- 1 tablespoon rice vinegar
- 1 tablespoon minced ginger
- 1/2 cup finely chopped broccoli
- 2 cloves garlic minced
- 1/2 cup frozen peas

Directions:

1. In a large bowl, crumble the tofu (you're going for scrambled egg-size pieces, not ricotta here), then toss with the rest of the Round 1 ingredients. Air fry at 370F for 10 minutes, shaking once.
2. Meanwhile, toss together all of the Round 2 ingredients in a large bowl*.
3. When that first 10 minutes of cooking are done, add all of the Round 2 ingredients to your air fryer, shake gently, and fry at 370 for 10 more minutes, shaking after 5 minutes.
4. Riced cauliflower can vary quite a bit in size, so if you feel like yours doesn't look done enough at this point, you can cook for an additional 2-5 minutes at 370F. Just shake and check in every couple of minutes until it's done to your liking.

Keto Air Fryer Fried Mushrooms

Ingredients:

- 2 cups sliced mushrooms
- 1 cup almond flour
- 2 eggs, beaten
- Salt / Pepper to taste
- 1/4 tsp oil in a spritzer

Directions:

1. Dip each mushroom slice in egg wash, followed by drenching them in almond flour with salt and pepper to taste.
2. Lightly spritz the bottom of the air fryer with oil.
3. Lay the mushrooms out in a single layer in your air fryer.
4. Spritz the mushrooms lightly with the oil.
5. Set your air fryer to 400 degrees F and cook for about 7 minutes, flipping halfway through.

Air Fryer 2 Ingredient Parmesan Zucchini Crisps

Servings: 2   **Cook Time: 12 Mins**   **Prep Time: 10 Mins**

Ingredients:

- 1 medium zucchini sliced into ¼ inch thick rounds
- ½ Cup grated parmesan cheese freshly grated

Directions:

1. Place zucchini rounds into your air fryer in a single layer. (If your air fryer basket is nonstick you don't need to grease the basket first. If it is not nonstick, you should spray basket with cooking oil spray.) Add a thin layer of parmesan cheese over rounds, covering the surface of each round.

2. Set your air fryer to 370°F (no preheat). Cook rounds for about 12 minutes, or until the cheese is dark golden brown. Let the rounds cool for a few minutes, which will allow the cheese to crisp up further.

3. Serve with your favorite dipping sauce. Crisps are best eaten soon after they are fried. Because of the moisture in the zucchini, the crispy top will soften when fully cooled. If you are making a large batch, you can always re-crisp them again in the air fryer.

Air Fryer Fried Parmesan Zucchini

Servings: 6 **Cook Time: 32 Mins** **Prep Time: 10 Mins**

Ingredients:

- 2 medium zucchini
- 1 large egg
- 1/2 cup grated parmesan cheese
- 1/4 cup almond flour
- 1/2 teaspoon garlic powder
- 1 teaspoon Italian seasoning
- Avocado oil spray or other cooking oil spray

Directions:

1. Slice zucchini into 1/4 to 1/3 of an inch slices.
2. Beat egg well in a separate bowl.
3. Combine grated parmesan cheese, almond flour, garlic powder and Italian seasoning in another bowl.
4. Dip zucchini slice in egg then dip it in the parmesan cheese mixture. Set on parchment lined air fryer tray.
5. Repeat until air fryer tray is full. Lightly spray coated zucchini with avocado oil spray.
6. Set air fryer to 370F for 8 minutes.
7. Remove tray and flip zucchini slices. Spray with avocado oil and cook for another 8 minutes.
8. Repeat process with second batch of zucchini.
9. Serve warm.

Air Fryer Garlic Mushrooms

Servings: 2   **Cook Time: 15 Mins**   **Prep Time: 10 Mins**

Ingredients:

- 8 oz. (227 g) mushrooms , washed and dried
- 1-2 Tablespoons (15-30 ml) olive oil
- 1/2 teaspoon (2.5 ml) garlic powder
- 1 teaspoon (5 ml) Worcestershire or soy sauce
- Kosher salt , to taste
- Black pepper , to taste
- Lemon wedges (optional)
- 1 Tablespoon (15 ml) chopped parsley
- Equipment
- Air fryer

Directions:

1. Cut mushrooms in half or quarters (depending on preferred size). Add to bowl then toss with oil, garlic powder, Worcestershire/soy sauce, salt and pepper
2. Air fry at 380°F for 10-12 minutes, tossing and shaking half way through.
3. Squeeze lemon and top with chopped parsley.

Air Fryer Apple Turnovers

Ingredients:

- 2 Bramley apples or 3 smaller varieties (Granny Smiths, Royal Galas)
- 2 tbsp + 1 tbsp brown sugar
- 1 tsp ground cinnamon
- 1 tbsp lemon juice
- 320g puff pastry
- 2 tbsp milk

Directions:

1. Peel the apples and dice them into equal sizes.
2. Mix with 2 tbsp brown sugar, 1 tsp ground cinnamon and 1 tbsp of lemon juice.
3. Place in air fryer basket and cook at 190°C/380°F for 10 minutes, shaking at the halfway mark. If you prefer a smoother filing, you can stew the apples in a saucepan on the hob instead.
4. Cut the puff pastry into four equal sizes and lay out on a floured surface.
5. Divide the cooked apple between each pastry piece and place it on one side, leaving about 1cm of space around the edge.
6. With a pastry brush, baste the edges of each puff pastry with some milk before folding it over.
7. Press the edges down with a fork until all sides are stuck firmly together.
8. Baste the top of the apple turnover with some milk and pierce a hole in the top to allow the steam to escape.
9. Transfer each apple turnover to the air fryer basket. If your air fryer basket is prone to sticking, spray a little oil on it or use some baking paper.
10. Air fry at the same temperature for 10 to 12 minutes, carefully flipping over halfway. The puff pastry should be golden brown and flaky when it's ready.

Air Fryer Apple Crumble

Servings: X **Cook Time: X Mins** **Prep Time: X Mins**

Ingredients:

- 2 large Bramley apples
- 225 g plain flour, (8oz)
- 115 g butter, (4oz)
- 80 g Sugar, (3oz)

Directions:

1. Preheat air fryer to 180C (350F)
2. Peel and chop apples into small chunks and place in air fryer safe baking tin.
3. In a mixing bowl, combine the flour and butter. Using your hands, rub it together until it resembles breadcrumbs.
4. Stir in the sugar.
5. Add crumble mixture on top of the apple chunks.
6. Place in air fryer basket for 18 minutes. Check at 15 minutes to make sure it isn't cooking too quickly. When the crumble is golden, it is ready.
7. Tastes great with custard or ice cream.

Air Fryer Halloumi

Servings: 8 **Cook Time: 8 Mins** **Prep Time: 2 Mins**

Ingredients:

- 225g halloumi
- 1 tbsp olive oil
- 1/2 tsp dried thyme (optional)

Directions:

1. Preheat the air fryer to 200°C (390°F).
2. Slice halloumi and brush with oil on both sides. Sprinkle with seasoning if using.
3. Transfer halloumi slices to the air fryer basket and air fry for 8 to 10 minutes, turning over halfway.
4. The halloumi is ready when it has softened and is beginning to turn brown around the edges.

Air Fryer Garlic Parmesan Asparagus

Ingredients:

- 1 pound asparagus
- 2 teaspoons olive oil
- 1/2 teaspoon garlic powder, can swap for some freshly minced garlic
- 1/2 lemon (juiced)
- Salt
- Ground pepper
- 1/4 cup Parmesan cheese (shredded or grated)

Directions:

1. Wash and either cut or snap off each end. Discard the ends.
2. Toss on olive oil, garlic powder and a pinch of salt and pepper. Squeeze half a lemon on and toss together to fully coat each asparagus.
3. Place in air fryer for 10 minutes on 390 degrees. Cook longer if desired.
4. Sprinkle with Parmesan cheese and serve

Air Fryer Cabbage Wedges With Bacon

Ingredients:

- 1 small head of green Cabbage
- 6 strips thick cut Bacon
- 1 tsp Onion Powder
- 1 tsp Garlic Powder
- 1/2 tsp Fennel Seeds
- 1/4 tsp Chili Flakes
- 3 tbsp Olive Oil optional
- Salt and pepper to taste

Directions:

1. Place the bacon slices in a well-greased air fryer basket
2. Air fry at 350F for 10 minutes. Chop it up and set it aside.
3. Remove the outer layer of the cabbage. Keeping the core intact cut the cabbages into wedges. Depending on the size of the cabbage, you will get 4, 6 or 8 wedges.
4. In a small bowl, combine the garlic powder, onion powder, fennel seeds, chili flakes (if using), salt and pepper.
5. Drizzle the cabbage wedges with oil and sprinkle both sides with the prepared spice mix.
6. Arrange the wedges in a well-greased air fryer basket and air fry at 400 for 8 minutes. Flip and drizzle with some ore oil and air fry again for 6 minutes.
7. Carefully take out the cabbages wedges. Top with chopped bacon and a little sprinkle of fresh herb of choice.
8. Serve warm as a side dish.

Chocolate and Chilli Brownies in the Airfryer

Ingredients:

- 200 g butter, melted
- 100 g cocoa powder
- 75 g dark chocolate, melted
- 2 large eggs
- 150 g caster sugar
- 1/2 tsp vanilla essence
- 150 g self-raising flour
- 1 level tbsp crushed dried chilli flakes

Directions:

1. Preheat airfryer to 180C/350F
2. Mix butter, sugar and crushed dried chillies.
3. Beat the eggs and mix them in. Add the melted chocolate and vanilla extract.
4. Slowly add in the flour and cocoa powder. Mix gently, do not over stir.
5. Using a greased, or baking paper lined tin/container, pour the mixture in.
6. Cook in the air fryer for 15 to 20 minutes, checking a few times to make sure the top isn't burning - if it is cooking quickly, put some foil or baking paper on top.
7. Once ready, allow to cool and then cut into smaller portions to serve.

Air Fryer Tofu

Servings: 4　　**Cook Time: 10 Mins**　　**Prep Time: 10 Mins**

Ingredients:

- 300g firm tofu
- 2 tbsp soy sauce
- 2 tsp sesame oil
- 2 tsp seasoning*
- 2 tbsp cornflour

Directions:

1. Cut the tofu into 1 inch size cubes using a sharp knife or kitchen scissors.
2. Place in a bowl and add the remaining ingredients, tossing everything together until the tofu is well coated.
3. Leave the tofu to marinate for 5 to 10 minutes. During this time, you can preheat the air fryer at 200C/400F.
4. Transfer the marinated tofu to the air fryer basket and cook for 10 minutes. Shake the basket at 5 minutes to ensure the tofu crisps all the way over.
5. Serve alone or with your favourite dip.

Notes

*seasoning - I used 2 tsp of season-all, but you can use any flavours, try garlic powder and paprika or a curry powder spice mix.

Air Fryer Boiled Eggs

Servings: 4   **Cook Time: 10 Mins**   **Prep Time: 1 Mins**

Ingredients:

- 4 eggs (cook as many as you need)

Directions:

1. Add room temperature eggs to the basket of your air fryer, and leave some space between them so that there is room for the hot air to circulate. Use a metal rack if needed to fit more in.
2. Set the air fryer temperature at 150C. Cook according to how well done you want your eggs (starting at 8 minutes for runny, up to 12 minutes for hard boiled).
3. At the end of the cooking time remove from the air fryer basket and plunge into an ice bath or into a bowl of cold water – this will prevent the eggs from continuing to cook.
4. Once they have cooled down a little and can be handled, remove the shell.

Air Fryer Meatballs

Servings: X   **Cook Time: 7 Mins**   **Prep Time: 10 Mins**

Ingredients:

- 500g lean beef mince, (1 pound)
- 1 clove garlic, crushed
- 1 tsp dried mixed herbs
- 1 egg
- 1tbsp breadcrumbs, (optional)

Directions:

1. Mix all ingredients together until well combined.
2. Using your hands, form small round balls (this recipe makes about 16, depending on size of meatballs)
3. Place meatballs in air fryer and cook at 180C/350F for 7 minutes. Check half way through and turn over if necessary.
4. If you want to add a sauce, once the meatballs are cooked transfer them to an ovenproof dish/pan that will fit in the Airfryer. Pour your choice of tomato sauce on top and place container in Airfryer tray. Cook at 180C/350F for about 6-8 minutes, or until the sauce is warmed through.
5. Serve with spaghetti and melted cheese.

Air Fryer Pizza

Ingredients:

- 240g (1 cup) natural or Greek yoghurt
- 350g (2 cups) self-raising flour
- grated cheese (enough to sprinkle on 2 small pizzas)
- pizza sauce/passata
- toppings of your choice (pepperoni, pineapple, peppers, chicken etc)

Directions:

1. Mix the self raising flour and yoghurt together (add more flour if necessary) until a dough consistency has been formed.
2. Split dough in 2.
3. Roll each one out on a floured surface.
4. Place on a bit of parchment paper in air fryer basket and cook at 200C/400F for 8 to 10 minutes, turning over half way.
5. Take pizza out and add pizza sauce, grated cheese & any other toppings of your choice.
6. Return to air fryer basket and cook for a further 3 minutes.
7. Repeat with 2nd pizza.

Air Fryer Pork & Turkey

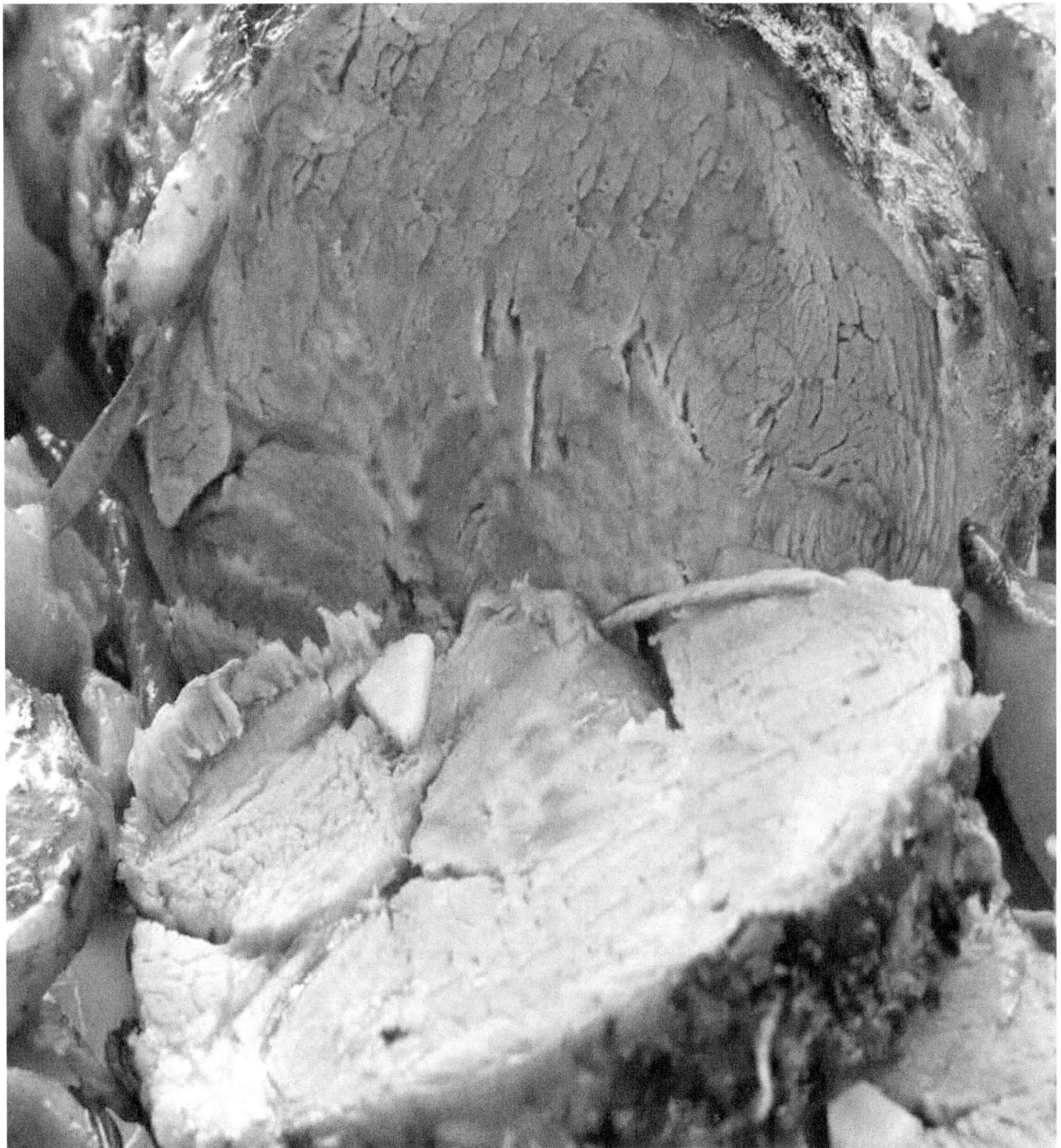

Air Fryer Pork Chops

Ingredients:

- 1 pork chop
- 1/2 tbsp olive oil
- 1/2 tbsp seasoning (see notes)

Directions:

1. Preheat the air fryer to 200C (400F).
2. Brush oil on each side of the pork chop.
3. Add seasoning and rub it in evenly all over.
4. Place pork chop in the preheated air fryer and set the timer for 12 minutes. Turn the pork chop over at around the 6 minute mark.
5. Check the pork chop is cooked all the way through - it should be golden brown on the outside and juices should run clear.

Notes

Pork Chops

You can air fry as many pork chops as you can fit in the air fryer - you might need to batch cook.

Seasoning

You can cook the pork chops without seasoning or add one of your favourites. Here are some options;

BBQ

Curried

Garlic and Herb

Peri Peri

Keto Pork Chops

Ingredients:

- 4 1-2 Inch Thick Boneless Pork Chops
- 1 3 Ounce Bag Pork Rinds, Crushed In The Food Processor
- 1 Teaspoon Kosher Salt
- 1 Teaspoon Smoked Paprika
- 1/2 Teaspoon Garlic Powder
- 1/2 Teaspoon Onion Powder
- 2 Large Eggs, Beaten

Directions:

1. In A Shallow Bowl, Mix The Crushed Pork Rinds With The Seasonings. In A Separate Shallow Bowl, Add In The Beaten Eggs. One At A Time, Coat The Pork Chops In The Egg, Then In The Pork Rind Mixture. Place The Breaded Pork Chops In The Air Fryer.
2. For 1 Inch Pork Chops, Set The Air Fryer At 400F For 12 Minutes And Flip Half Way Through. For 2 Inch Thick Pork Chops, Set The Air Fryer For 20 Minutes And Cook Half Way Through. Pork Chops Are Done When An Internal Temperature Thermometer Reads 145-160F.

Oven

3. Place The Breaded Pork Chops On A Sheet Tray And Bake In A 425F Oven For 15 Minutes On Each Side Or Until An Internal Meat Thermometer Reads 145F.

Air Fryer Baby Back Ribs

Servings: 4   **Cook Time: 20 Mins**   **Prep Time: 5 Mins**

Ingredients:

- 1 Rack Of Baby Back Ribs, Cut Ribs Into Sections
- 1 Tbsp. Liquid Smoke
- 1 Tbsp. Oil
- Seasoning:
- 2 Teaspoons Kosher Salt
- 1 Teaspoon Ground Black Pepper
- 1 Teaspoon Chili Powder
- 1 Teaspoon Onion Powder
- ½ Teaspoon Garlic Powder
- ½ Teaspoon Brown Sugar (Add Low Carb Sugar If You Are Keto Such As Truvia Brown Sugar Blend)

Directions:

1. Pat The Ribs Dry With Kitchen Paper Towel Then Rub All Over Oil And Liquid Smoke.
2. Mix All The Ingredients For Seasoning Together. Season The Ribs With The Spices.
3. Cut The Rack Of Ribs Into Sections 4-5 Ribs To Fit The Air Fryer.
4. Cook The Ribs In The Air Fryer For 20 To 40 Minutes At 400 Degrees Fahrenheit, Depending On The Rib Thickens As Well As Your Air Fryer.
5. After The Ribs Are Done, You May Brush Some BBQ Sauce And Pop In The Air Fryer For 5 More Minutes, But It Is Not Necessary. I Like Brushing Just The Leftover Drippings For More Flavorful Ribs.
6. If You Do Not Want To Add BBQ Sauce Then Just Allow The Ribs To Rest For About 10 Min So The Juices Could Go Back.

Crispy Air Fryer Pork Chops

| Servings: 6 | Cook Time: 12 Mins | Prep Time: 5 Mins |

Ingredients:

- 1 1/2 Lb Boneless Pork Chops
- 1/3 Cup Almond Flour
- 1/4 Cup Grated Parmesan Cheese
- 1 Tsp Garlic Powder
- 1 Tsp Tony Chachere's Creole Seasoning
- 1 Tsp Paprika

Directions:

1. Preheat Your Air Fryer To 360 Degrees F
2. Meanwhile, Combine All Ingredients EXCEPT Pork Chops Into A Large Ziplock Bag.
3. Place The Pork Chops Into The Bag, Seal It, And Then Shake To Coat The Pork Chops.
4. Remove From The Bag And Place In The Air Fryer In A Single Layer. Cook For 8-12 Minutes Depending Upon The Thickness Of Your Pork Chops.

Air Fryer Bacon

| Servings: 11 | Cook Time: 11 Mins | Prep Time: X Mins |

Ingredients:

- 11 Slices Bacon (I Am Using Trader Joe's, And It Is A Thick-Cut Bacon)

Directions:

1. Divide The Bacon Strips In Half, And Place The First Half In The Air Fryer In A Single Layer.
2. Set The Temperature At 400 Degrees, And Set The Timer To 10 Minutes (Possibly Less Time For Thinner Bacon).
3. Check It Halfway Through To See If Anything Needs To Be Rearranged (Tongs Are Helpful!).
4. Cook Remainder Of The Time. Check For Desired Doneness. I Like Mine Extra Crispy So I Did About 1.5 Minutes Extra For A Total Of 11.5 Minutes, And Mine Was Perfect.
5. Use Tongs To Place Finished Cooked Bacon On Paper Towels To Drain Excess Grease.

Best Damn Air Fryer Pork Loin Roast

Servings: 6   **Cook Time: 55-65 Mins**   **Prep Time: X Mins**

Ingredients:

- 2lb – 2 1/2lb Boneless Pork Loin Roast
- 1 Tbs Brown Sugar
- 1 Tbs Smoked Paprika
- 1 1/2 Tsp Ground Mustard
- 1 Tsp Onion Powder
- 1 Tsp Garlic Powder
- 1 Tsp Black Pepper
- 1 Tsp Course Salt
- 1/4 Tsp Cayenne (Optional)
- 1 Tbs Olive Oil

Directions:

1. Mix All Dry Ingredients In A Bowl
2. Coat The Roast With Olive Oil And Add The Seasoning Rub. Massage It Well Onto The Entire Roast.
3. Preheat Air Fryer To 360° F For 5 Minutes. After 5 Minutes, Carefully Place Pork Roast Into Air Fryer And Air Fry At 360° F For 45-55 Minutes. Internal Temp Should Be 145° – 160° F. (If Internal Temperature Is Not Yet 145°, Continue To Cook Another 5-10 Minutes Or However Long Is Required Depending On Weight Of Roast)

Air Fryer Turkey Breast

Ingredients:

- 4 Pound Turkey Breast (On The Bone With Skin (Ribs Removed))
- 1 Tablespoon Olive Oil
- 2 Teaspoons Kosher
- 1/2 Tablespoon Dry Turkey Or Poultry Seasoning (I Used Bell's Which Has Not Salt)

Directions:

1. Rub 1/2 Tablespoon Of Oil All Over The Turkey Breast. Season Both Sides With Salt And Turkey Seasoning Then Rub In The Remaining Half Tablespoon Of Oil Over The Skin Side.
2. Preheat The Air Fryer 350F And Cook Skin Side Down 20 Minutes, Turn Over And Cook Until The Internal Temperature Is 160F Using An Instant-Read Thermometer About 30 To 40 Minutes More Depending On The Size Of Your Breast. Let Is Rest 10 Minutes Before Carving.

Air Fryer Crustless Pizza

Servings: 4   **Cook Time: 10 Mins**   **Prep Time: 10 Mins**

Ingredients:

- 1 Lbs Cooked Ground Beef Browned And Drained
- 2 Cups Shredded Mozzarella Cheese Divided
- 7 Oz Marinara Sauce
- Your Favorite Pizza Toppings

Directions:

1. Put Your Beef And 1 Cup Mozzarella In A Bowl And Mix It Together
2. Evenly Spread Out Your Beef Mixture In Your Pizza Or Barrel Pan.
3. Pour Your Marinara Sauce Across The Top And Spread Out Evenly
4. Top With Remaining Cheese And Toppings. Note: If Using Pepperonis, Add A Bit Of Cheese On Top Of Them Or They May Take Flight During Cooking!
5. Place Pan In Air Fryer Basket (Or On Trivet If Using Mealthy Crisplid)
6. Air Fry At 360 (Or 350 If Unable To Set To 360) For 10 Minutes And Check For Desired Crispness Of Cheese. Crispy Cheese Lovers May Enjoy Pizzas Cooked Up To 15 Minutes.

Keto Air Fryer Bone-In Pork Chops

Ingredients:

- 4 Bone In Pork Chops About ¼-Inch Thick
- 1 Tsp Parsley
- 1 Tsp Paprika
- 1/8 Tsp All Spice
- 1 Tsp Onion Powder
- 1 Tsp Garlic Powder
- 2 Cups Finely Crushed Pork Rinds Finely Crushed
- Olive Oil

Directions:

1. In A Medium Size Bowl (Needs To Be Big Enough To Dip The Pork Chops Iadd Pork Rinds, Parsley, Paprika, Onion And Garlic Powders And All Spice. Whisk Until Combined.
2. Drizzle Each Pork Chop On Both Sides With Olive Oil, Ensuring To Cover It All As The Pork Rinds Are Going To Stick To The Olive Oil.
3. Place Each Pork Chop In The Pork Rind Mixture, Coating It Entirely On Both Sides.
4. Place Pork Chops In Air Fryer, Ensuring Not To Over Crowd.
5. Set Air Fryer To 400° For 12 Minutes. Once Done Flip The Pork Chop Over And Cook For Another 5 Minutes At 400°.

Air Fryer Sausage

Ingredients:

- 1 Pkg Uncooked Italian Sausage, Mild, Sweet, Or Hot

Directions:

1. Since Italian Sausages Are Already Preseasoned And Have A Higher Fat Content, You Don't Need To Do Any Prep Work For This Recipe. I Like To Take The Sausage Out Of The Fridge For 5-10 Minutes Before Cooking.
2. Air Fryer Italian Sausage Temperature
3. Cook On 360 F.
4. Lay The Sausage In A Single Layer On The Air Fryer Basket, Leaving Room On All Sides.
5. No Need To Preheat The Air Fryer, Just Lay The Sausages On The Basket And Put In At 360 F.
6. Air Fry Sausage Cook Time
7. Cook The Italian Sausages In An Air Fryer Oven For 6 Minutes Flip Over, And Continue Cooking For 5-6 Minutes, Or Until The Internal Temperature Reaches 160F. Some Air Fryer Models Could Take Slightly Longer To Cook.
8. Be Sure Not To Overcook The Sausages As They'll Start To Shrivel And Juices Could Start Leaking Out Of The Sausage.
9. Remove The Italian Sausages From The Air Fryer And Let Rest For 5 Minutes Before Serving. It Takes At Least 5 Minutes For The Juices To Redistribute Evenly Throughout The Meat And Make Every Bite Juicy And Moist.
10. Enjoy!

Air Fryer Pork Chops and Broccoli

Ingredients:

- 2 5 Ounce Bone-In Pork Chops
- 2 Tablespoons Avocado Oil, Divided
- 1/2 Teaspoon Paprika
- 1/2 Teaspoon Onion Powder
- 1/2 Teaspoon Garlic Powder
- 1 Teaspoon Salt, Divided
- 2 Cups Broccoli Florets
- 2 Cloves Garlic, Minced

Directions:

1. Preheat Air Fryer According To Manufacturer's Instructions To 350 Degrees. Spray Basket With Non-Stick Spray.
2. Drizzle 1 Tablespoon Of Oil Both Sides Of The Pork Chops.
3. Season The Pork Chops On Both Sides With The Paprika, Onion Powder, Garlic Powder, And 1/2 Teaspoon Of Salt.
4. Place Pork Chops In The Air Fryer Basket And Cook For 5 Minutes.
5. While Pork Chops Are Cooking, Add The Broccoli, Garlic, Remaining 1/2 Teaspoon Of Salt, And Remaining Tablespoon Of Oil To A Bowl And Toss To Coat.
6. Open The Air Fryer And Carefully Flip The Pork Chops.
7. Add The Broccoli To The Basket And Return To The Air Fryer.
8. Cook For 5 More Minutes, Stirring The Broccoli Halfway Through.
9. Carefully Remove The Food From The Air Fryer And Serve.

Air Fryer Ribs

Servings: 4 **Cook Time: 10 Mins** **Prep Time: 40 Mins**

Ingredients:

- 1 Tablespoon Sesame Oil
- 1 Teaspoon Minced Garlic
- 1 Teaspoon Minced Ginger
- 1 Tablespoon Fermented Black Bean Paste
- 1 Tablespoon Shaoxing Wine
- 1 Tablespoon Dark Soy Sauce
- 1 Tablespoon Agave Nectar Or Honey
- 1.5 Pounds Spare Ribs Cut Into Small Pieces

Directions:

1. In A Large Mixing Bowl, Stir Together All Ingredients For The Marinade.
2. Add The Spare Ribs And Mix Well. Allow The Ribs To Marinade For At Least 30 Minutes Or Up To 24 Hours.
3. When You're Ready To Cook The Ribs, Remove The Ribs From The Marinade And Place Into The Air Fryer Basket.
4. Set The Air Fryer At 375F For 8 Minutes.
5. Check To Ensure The Ribs Have An Internal Temperature Of 165F Before Serving.

Crispy Keto Parmesan Crusted Pork Chops In The Air Fryer

Servings 4 · Cook Time: 16 Mi · Tim Mins

Servings: 4 · **Cook Time: 15 Mins** · **Prep Time: 5 Mins**

Ingredients:

- 4 To 6 Thick Center Cut Boneless Pork Chops These Are My Favorite But You Can Use The Bone-In Pork Chops Also
- 1/2 Tsp Salt
- 1/4 Tsp Pepper
- 1 Tsp Smoked Paprika
- 1/2 Tsp Onion Powder
- 1/4 Tsp Chili Powder
- 2 Large Eggs Beaten
- 1 Cup Pork Rind Crumbs
- 3 Tbs Grated Parmesan Cheese

Directions:

1. Preheat The Air Fryer To 400F For About 10 Minutes.
2. Season Both Sides Of Each Pork Chop With Salt And Pepper.
3. Use A Food Processor To Blend The Pork Rinds Into Crumbs.
4. Combine The Pork Rind Crumbs And Seasonings In A Large Bowl.
5. Place The Beaten Egg In A Separate Bowl.
6. Dip Each Pork Chop Into The Egg Mixture First, Then The Crumb Mixture Immediately After.
7. Place Each Pork Chop In The Basket.
8. Cook Them At 400 Degrees For 12 To 15 Minutes. 15 Minutes For The Really Thick Pork Chops. I Am Usually Able To Fit About 4 Or 5 Pork Chops In The Basket Of The Air Fryer At A Time.

Air Fryer Salmon

Air Fryer Crab Cakes Recipe

Ingredients:

- Crab Cakes
- 8 ounces lump crab meat (canned is fine, but drain well)
- 1/4 cup almond flour
- 2 tbsp chopped fresh parsley
- 1 green onion, sliced
- 1/2 tsp Old Bay seasoning (or other fish seasoning)
- 1/2 tsp salt
- 1/4 tsp pepper
- 1 large egg
- 1 tbsp mayonnaise
- 2 tsp Dijon mustard
- 2 tbsp melted butter
- Spicy Mayo
- 1/4 cup mayonnaise
- 1 tsp sriracha
- 1/2 tsp Cajun seasoning (more to taste - it can be very salty)

Directions:

1. In a large bowl, break up the crab meat with a fork. Stir in the almond flour, parsley, green onion, Old Bay, salt, and pepper until well combined.
2. Stir in the egg, mayo, and mustard until the mixture is well moistened. Use your hands to form into 4 patties, each about ¾ inch to 1 inch thick. Place on a waxed paper lined plate and refrigerate at least 30 minutes.
3. Spray or brush the air fryer rack with oil (I used avocado oil spray). Brush melted butter over both sides of the crab cakes and place on the rack.
4. Air fry at 350F for 10 minutes, carefully flipping halfway through cooking.
5. For the mayo, whisk the ingredients together in a small bowl. Serve the crab cakes with lemon and a dollop of spicy mayo.

Keto Air Fryer Fish Sticks

Servings: 4   **Cook Time: 10 Mins**   **Prep Time: 10 Mins**

Ingredients:

- 1 lb white fish such as cod
- 1/4 cup mayonnaise
- 2 tbsp Dijon mustard
- 2 tbsp water
- 1 1/2 cups pork rind panko such as Pork King Good
- 3/4 tsp cajun seasoning
- Salt and pepper to taste

Directions:

1. Spray the air fryer rack with non-stick cooking spray (I use avocado oil spray).
2. Pat the fish dry and cut into sticks about 1 inch by 2 inches wide (how you are able to cut it will depend a little on what kind of fish you by and how thick and wide it is).
3. In a small shallow bowl, whisk together the mayo, mustard, and water. In another shallow bowl, whisk together the pork rinds and Cajun seasoning. Add salt and pepper to taste (both the pork rinds and seasoning could have a fair bit of salt so dip a finger in to taste how salty it is).
4. Working with one piece of fish at a time, dip into the mayo mixture to coat and then tap off the excess. Dip into the pork rind mixture and toss to coat. Place on the air fryer rack.
5. Set to Air Fry at 400F and bake 5 minutes, the flip the fish sticks with tongs and bake another 5 minutes. Serve immediately.

Perfect Air Fryer Salmon

Servings: 2   **Cook Time: 7 Mins**   **Prep Time: 2 Mins**

Ingredients:

- 2 wild caught salmon fillets with comparable thickness, mine were 1-1/12-inches thick
- 2 tsps teaspoons avocado oil or olive oil
- 2 tsps paprika
- generously seasoned with salt and coarse black pepper
- lemon wedges

Directions:

1. Remove any bones from your salmon if necessary and let fish sit on the counter for an hour. Rub each fillet with olive oil and season with paprika, salt and pepper.
2. Place fillets in the basket of the air fryer. Set air fryer at 390 degrees for 7 minutes for 1-1/2-inch fillets.
3. When timer goes off, open basket and check fillets with a fork to make sure they are done to your desired doneness.

Paleo Air Fryer Salmon Patties

Servings: 4   **Cook Time: 15 Mins**   **Prep Time: 35 Mins**

Ingredients:

- 1 lb ALDI Fresh Atlantic Salmon Side (half a side)
- 1/4 Cup Avocado, mashed
- 1/4 Cup Cilantro, diced + additional for garnish
- 1 1/2 tsp Yellow curry powder
- 1/2 tsp Stonemill Sea Salt Grinder
- 1/4 Cup + 4 tsp Tapioca Starch, divided (40g)
- 2 SimplyNature Organic Cage Free Brown Eggs
- 1/2 Cup SimplyNature Organic Coconut Flakes (30g)
- SimplyNature Organic Coconut Oil, melted (for brushing)
- For the greens:
- 2 tsp SimplyNature Organic Coconut Oil, melted
- 6 Cups SimplyNature Organic Arugula & Spinach Mix, tightly packed
- Pinch of Stonemill Sea Salt Grinder

Directions:

1. Remove the skin from the salmon, dice the flesh, and add it into a large bowl.
2. Add in the avocado, cilantro, curry powder, sea salt and stir until well mixed. Then, stir in 4 tsp of the tapioca starch until well incorporated.
3. Line a baking sheet with parchment paper. Form the salmon into 8, 1/4 cup-sized patties, just over 1/2 inch thick, and place them onto the pan. Freeze for 20 minutes so they are easier to work with.
4. While the patties freeze, pre-heat your Air Fryer to 400 degrees for 10 minutes, rubbing the basket with coconut oil. Additionally, whisk the eggs and place them into a shallow plate. Place the remaining 1/4 cup of Tapioca starch and the coconut flakes in separate shallow plates as well.
5. Once the patties have chilled, dip one into the tapioca starch, making sure it's fully covered. Then, dip it into the egg, covering it entirely, and gently brushing off any excess. Finally, press just the top and sides of the cake into the coconut flakes and place it, coconut flake-side up, into the air fryer. Repeat with all cakes. **
6. Gently brush the tops with a little bit of melted coconut oil (optional, but recommended) and cook until the outside is golden brown and crispy, and the inside is juicy and tender, about 15 minutes. Note: the patties will stick to the Air Fryer basked a little, so use a sharp-edged spatula to remove them.
7. When the cakes have about 5 minutes left to cook, heat the coconut oil up in a large pan on medium heat. Add in the Arugula and Spinach Mix, and a pinch of salt, and cook, stirring constantly, until the greens JUST begin to wilt, only 30 seconds - 1 minute.
8. Divide the greens between 4 plates, followed by the salmon cakes. Garnish with extra cilantro and DEVOUR!
9. If you want to bake in the oven:
10. Preheat your oven to 400 degrees and line a baking sheet with parchment paper, placing a cooling rack on top of the pan. Rub the cooling rack with coconut oil.
11. Place the patties, coconut-side up, onto the cooling rack and bake for 15-17 minutes until crispy. NOTE: we liked these better in the air fryer, as they do get a little crispier, but they are still good in the oven!

Perfect Air Fryer Salmon

Ingredients:

- 2 wild caught salmon fillets with comparable thickness, mine were 1-1/12-inches thick
- 2 tsps teaspoons avocado oil or olive oil
- 2 tsps paprika
- generously seasoned with salt and coarse black pepper
- lemon wedges

Directions:

1. Remove any bones from your salmon if necessary and let fish sit on the counter for an hour. Rub each fillet with olive oil and season with paprika, salt and pepper.
2. Place fillets in the basket of the air fryer. Set air fryer at 390 degrees for 7 minutes for 1-1/2-inch fillets.
3. When timer goes off, open basket and check fillets with a fork to make sure they are done to your desired doneness.

Notes

One of the beauties of the air fryer is that it's so easy to pop something back in for a minute if you want it cooked longer. You can also open it while it's cooking to make sure it's not overdone. I always set my timer for a little less so I can check on how things are coming along so I don't overcook an item. Things cook so fast sometimes a minute more is all it needs.

Times for cooking will vary for salmon based on the temperature of the fish and the size of your fillets. Always set your air fryer for a little less time than you think until you become more used to the timing of your appliance.

Air Fryer Salmon

Servings: X **Cook Time: 10 Mins** **Prep Time: 5 Mins**

Ingredients:

- 2 salmon fillets
- 1/2 tbsp olive oil
- Salt and pepper to season

Directions:

1. Switch air fryer on and set the temperature to 200C (400F).
2. Rub a little oil on each salmon fillet and season with salt and pepper or your favourite seasoning or marinade.
3. Lightly spray the air fryer basket with a little oil and place the salmon fillets in the basket.
4. Cook for 8 minutes. Check at this time to see if they are cooked - they should flake quite easily when they are ready. Cook for a further 1 to 2 minutes if necessary.

Air Fryer Appetizers

Keto Cauliflower Wings

Servings: 6 **Cook Time: 10 Mins** **Prep Time: 20 Mins**

Ingredients:

- Crispy cauliflower
- 1 head cauliflower
- 3 eggs beaten
- 3/4 cup almond flour
- 3/4 cup finely grated Parmesan cheese
- 1 teaspoon garlic powder
- 1/2 teaspoon smoked paprika
- Salt and Pepper to taste; I used ½ teaspoon each

Sauce

- 1 cup Frank's Red Hot Sauce
- 4 tablespoons butter

Directions:

1. Preheat your air fryer to 400 degrees or oven to 420.
2. Core the cauliflower and cut into larger florets.
3. Beat the eggs together in a small bowl.
4. In a separate bowl, combine the almond flour, Parmesan, garlic powder, smoked paprika, salt and pepper.
5. Dip the cauliflower into the egg mixture, and then coat in the almond flour mixture.
6. Transfer to a parchment lined baking sheet until ready to cook.
7. Continue with the remaining cauliflower.
8. Spray the bottom of your air fryer or a parchment lined baking sheet with oil.
9. Add the cauliflower in a single layer. Spray the top.
10. Cook for 10 to 12 minutes in the air fryer or 20 to 22 minutes in the oven, until golden brown, flipping half way through.
11. Sauce
12. While the cauliflower is cooking, make the sauce by combining the Franks Hot Sauce and butter in a small saucepan.
13. Heat over medium low heat until the butter melts.
14. To combine
15. Toss the crispy cauliflower with the sauce, and serve using a slotted spoon.

Air Fryer Chips

Ingredients:

- 600g potatoes
- Oil (optional)
- Seasoning

Directions:

1. Slice the potatoes up - thick for regular chips, or thin for French fries. You can either peel the potatoes, or give them a good scrub and leave the skin on.
2. Preheat air fryer to 200C/400F
3. Wash them in cold water to remove the starch.
4. Pat dry with kitchen towel or a tea towel.
5. Optionally spray with some oil.
6. Sprinkle with seasoning of your choice (chip seasoning, curry powder, paprika, salt and pepper).
7. Transfer to the air fryer basket.
8. Cook for 20 to 25 minutes, checking regularly and shaking/turning. Depending on the thickness of the chip, or how crispy you like them, you might want to cook them for longer.

Notes

9. The best potatoes for chips are Maris Pipers, King Edwards and Rooster.

Air Fryer Avocado Fries

Servings: 4   **Cook Time: 10 Mins**   **Prep Time: 10 Mins**

Ingredients:

- 2 avocados, slightly under ripe, this makes them easier to slice
- 1/3 cup almond flour
- 1 1/2 cups pork rinds, crushed
- 2 eggs, beaten
- 2 tbsp heavy cream
- 1/2 tsp paprika
- 1/2 tsp garlic powder
- 1/2 tsp salt & pepper
- 1/4 tsp each cumin and cayenne, optional

Directions:

1. Note, you will need 3 bowls or dishes for dredging
2. Peel avocado skin and slice long ways, evenly
3. Whisk cream and eggs together in one bowl
4. Combine almond flour and seasoning in one bowl
5. Add crushed pork rinds to one bowl
6. Dip avocado slice into the almond flour mixture coating evenly, then into the egg, then the pork rinds.
7. Place coated avocado slice into air fryer in a single layer.
8. Set air fryer at 400° for 5 minutes.
9. Flip avocado fries.
10. Set timer for 4-5 minutes. Remove.
11. Serve with your favorite dipping sauce or eat plain.

Low Carb Mozzarella Sticks

Ingredients:

- 12 Mozzarella sticks string cheese, cut in half
- 2 large Eggs beaten
- 1/2 cup Almond flour
- 1/2 cup Parmesan cheese the powdered kind
- 1 teaspoon Italian seasoning
- 1/2 teaspoon Garlic Salt

Directions:

1. In a bowl combine almond flour, Parmesan cheese, Italian seasoning, and garlic salt.
2. In a separate bowl whisk eggs.
3. One at a time coat your mozzarella stick halves in egg and then toss in the coating mixture. As you finish place them in a resealable container. If you have to make more than 1 layer place parchment paper between the layers of mozzarella sticks.
4. Freeze mozzarella sticks for 30 minutes.
5. Remove from freezer and place in Philips airfryer.
6. Set to 400 degrees F and cook for 5 minutes.
7. Open air fryer and let stand for 1 minute before moving low carb mozzarella sticks to a plate.

Jicama Fries In The Air Fryer

Ingredients:

- 8 cups Jicama (peeled and cut into fries, about 1/3 to 1/2 inch thick and 3 to 4 inches long)
- 2 tbsp Olive oil
- 1/2 tsp Garlic powder
- 1 tsp Cumin
- 1 tsp Sea salt
- 1/4 tsp Black pepper

Directions:

1. Boil a large pot of water on the stove. Add the jicama fries and boil for 18 to 25 minutes, until color becomes slightly translucent (instead of bright white) and no longer crunchy. Time will vary depending on the thickness of your fries.
2. When the jicama is not crunchy anymore, remove and pat dry.
3. Set the air fryer oven to 400 degrees (204 degrees C) and let it preheat for 2 to 3 minutes.
4. Place the fries into a large bowl. Drizzle with olive oil and season with garlic powder, cumin, and sea salt. Toss to coat.
5. Working in batches to avoid crowding, arrange jicama in the air fryer basket in a single layer, preferably with the pieces not touching each other. Air fry jicama fries for 10-12 minutes, until golden. Repeat with remaining fries.

Air Fryer Zucchini Fries Recipe

Servings: 6 **Cook Time: 10 Mins** **Prep Time: 15 Mins**

Ingredients:

ZUCCHINI FRIES

- 2 medium zucchini
- 1/2 cup flour
- 3 eggs
- Kosher salt and freshly ground black pepper
- 1/2 cup panko bread crumbs
- 1/2 cup Italian bread crumbs
- 1/4 cup parmesan cheese
- 1 Tablespoon extra virgin olive oil

LEMON TARRAGON AIOLI

- 1 egg
- 2 cloves garlic minced
- 1 Tablespoon lemon juice plus 1 teaspoon lemon zest
- 1/2 cup canola oil
- Kosher salt and freshly ground black pepper
- 2 Tablespoons minced fresh tarragon leaves

Directions:

ZUCCHINI FRIES:

1. Cut the zucchini into sticks no more than 1/2 inch thick and 3 inches long.
2. Add the flour to a shallow bowl. In a separate shallow bowl whisk the egg and season with salt and pepper. In a third shallow bowl, combine the panko, bread crumbs, parmesan cheese and olive oil.
3. Dredge zucchini in flour, then eggs, then Panko mixture.
4. Heat air fryer to 400 degrees.
5. Working in batches, place the zucchini fries in a single layer in the air fryer. Cook for 8-10 minutes, until crispy. Season with kosher salt while warm.

LEMON TARRAGON AIOLI:

6. While the fries cooking, prepare the aioli.
7. Combine egg, garlic, and lemon juice in a blender or food processor. With the motor running, slowly drizzle in the canola oil until emulsified.
8. Fold in the tarragon leaves and lemon zest and season with salt and pepper, to taste.

NOTES

9. Zucchini Fries can be reheated in the air fryer at 400 degrees for 3 minutes.
10. Lemon Tarragon Aioli can be stored in a sealed container in the refrigerator for up to 2 weeks.

Oil-Free Air Fryer Chips

Servings: X   **Cook Time: 30 Mins**   **Prep Time: X Mins**

Ingredients:

- 2 Large Red Potatoes
- 2 tsp salt
- 4 garlic cloves crushed or minced
- 2 tbsp homemade vegan parmesan

Directions:

1. Thinly slice the potatoes. I recommend using a mandolin (I use a 1.5mm blade.)
2. Place the sliced potatoes in a bowl and fill with water. Mix in 2 teaspoons of salt. Let soak for 30 minutes.
3. Drain and rinse the potatoes. Pat dry.
4. Toss the potatoes with crushed garlic and vegan parmesan.
5. Layer half of the potato slices in the air fryer, in no more than 4 or so layers. Don't overload the air fryer or the chips won't cook evenly.
6. Fry at 170 degrees Fahrenheit for 20-25 minutes, or until dry to the touch and no longer flimsy. Stir and toss the basket every 5 minutes or so.
7. Bump the temperature up to 400 degrees Fahrenheit and fry for an additional 5 minutes or until the potatoes have become crunchy.
8. Remove from the air fryer and top with more vegan parm or salt.
9. Repeat for the other half of the potato slices.
10. Snack away!

Crispy Air Fryer Kale Chips Recipe

Servings: 2   **Cook Time: X Mins**   **Prep Time: X Mins**

Ingredients:

- 4 cups loosely packed kale stemmed
- 2 teaspoons olive oil
- Pinch of salt
- 1-2 tablespoons seasoning mix of your choice.

Directions:

1. Lightly massage the kale with the oil and salt in a medium-sized bowl. You aren't going for a kale salad here, just a little wilting is fine. Then, dump the coated kale into the basket of your air fryer.
2. Cook on 370° F for 4-6 minutes (do not preheat), shaking every 2 minutes, checking for doneness. Check in every minute for the last 2 minutes.
3. Toss with your seasoning of choice, and eat immediately. These will get soggy, if you try to store them.

Air Fryer Sweet Potato

Servings: 3   **Cook Time: 35 Mins**   **Prep Time: 5 Mins**

Ingredients:

- 3 sweet potatoes
- 1 tablespoon olive oil
- 1-2 teaspoons kosher salt

Directions:

1. Wash your sweet potatoes and then create air holes with a fork in the potatoes.
2. Sprinkle them with the olive oil & salt, then rub evenly on the potatoes.
3. Once the potatoes are coated place them into the basket for the Air Fryer and place into the machine.
4. Cook your potatoes at 392 degrees for 35-40 minutes or until fork tender.
5. Top with your favorites!

Air Fryer Mozzarella Sticks

Ingredients:

- 1 (10 oz) package part skim mozzarella string cheese each stick cut in half
- 1/4 cup whole wheat flour
- 1 large egg
- 1/4 cup breadcrumbs
- 1/4 cup panko
- 1/2 - 1 teaspoon onion powder*
- 1/2 - 1 teaspoon garlic powder*
- 1/2 - 1 teaspoon salt*
- 1/2 - 1 teaspoon chili powder*
- 1/2 - 1 teaspoon smoked paprika*
- Marinara sauce for dipping
- Ranch for dipping

Directions:

1. Place halved cheese sticks into a ziplock baggie and place in freezer until frozen, at least 30 minutes.
2. Place egg into a shallow bowl and whisk until broken up. Set aside.
3. Place breadcrumbs, panko, onion powder, garlic powder, salt, chili powder, and smoked paprika in another shallow bowl and whisk until well combined. Set aside.
4. Line a rimmed baking sheet with a silicone mat or parchment paper.
5. Place frozen cheese sticks and flour into another ziplock baggie (the one from the freezer will have too many ice chunks) and shake until the cheese sticks and fully coated in the flour.
6. Discard excess flour.
7. Dunk one cheese stick in egg until fully coated and then in panko mixture until fully coated.
8. Place on lined baking sheet and repeat with remaining cheese sticks.
9. Place baking sheet in freezer until all the cheese sticks have re-frozen, at least an hour.
10. Preheat air fryer to 370 degrees F and grease the basket with cooking spray.
11. Place in the mozzarella sticks, work with about 6 at a time, so you don't over crowd them.
12. Close the air fryer and cook for 5 minutes.
13. Repeat with as many mozzarella sticks as you'd like. Store uncooked leftovers in the freezer!
14. Serve with dipping sauces and enjoy!

Notes

15. Use 1 teaspoon each of spice if you want a more aggressively seasoned mozzarella stick!
16. If you'd like to make these ahead of time, after the mozzarella sticks are frozen on the baking sheet, move them to a ziplock baggie and store in freezer for 2-3 months.

Easy Air Fryer Jalapeno Poppers

Ingredients:

- 10 fresh jalapenos
- 6 oz cream cheese I used reduced-fat
- 1/4 cup shredded cheddar cheese
- 2 slices bacon cooked and crumbled
- Cooking oil spray

Directions:

1. Slice the jalapenos in half, vertically, to create 2 halves per jalapeno.
2. Place the cream cheese in a bowl. Microwave for 15 seconds to soften.
3. Remove the seeds and the inside of the jalapeno. (Save some of the seeds if you prefer spicy poppers)
4. Combine the cream cheese, crumbled bacon, and shredded cheese in a bowl. Mix well.
5. For extra spicy poppers, add some of the seeds as noted above to the cream cheese mixture, and mix well.
6. Stuff each of the jalapenos with the cream cheese mixture.
7. Load the poppers into the Air Fryer. Spray the poppers with cooking oil.
8. Close the Air Fryer. Cook the poppers on 370 degrees for 5 minutes to 8 minutes.
9. Remove from the Air Fryer and cool before serving.

Air Fryer Keto Onion Rings Recipe

Servings: 4   **Cook Time: 16 Mins**   **Prep Time: 10 Mins**

Ingredients:

- 1 large Onion (sliced into rings 1/2 inch thick)
- 3 tbsp Wholesome Yum Coconut Flour
- 1/4 tsp Sea salt
- 2 large Eggs
- 2/3 cup Pork rinds (~1.8 oz)
- 3 tbsp Wholesome Yum Blanched Almond Flour
- 1/2 tsp Paprika
- 1/2 tsp Garlic powder

Directions:

1. Arrange 3 small, shallow bowls in a line:
2. Coconut flour and sea salt, stirred together
3. Eggs, beaten
4. Pork rinds, almond flour, paprika, and garlic powder, stirred together
5. Lightly grease 2 air fryer oven racks or an air fryer basket.
6. Dredge an onion ring in coconut flour. Dip it in the egg, shake off the excess, then place in the pork rind mixture. Scoop extra pork rind mixture over it, so that it's coated on all size. Place into the air fryer rack or basket. Repeat with all the onion rings, placing them in a single layer without touching. (You may need to cook them in two batches if you don't have 2 air fryer racks.)
7. Preheat the air fryer or air fryer oven to 400 degrees F for 2 to 3 minutes.
8. For an air fryer oven: Place both racks into the air fryer oven. Bake for about 8 minutes, until the top layer is golden. Switch racks and bake for 8 more minutes, until the top layer is golden again.
9. For a regular air fryer: Only half the onion rings will fit into the basket in a single layer. Place the basket into the air fryer. Bake for 16 minutes, until golden. Remove the onion rings, arrange the next batch of uncooked rings, and repeat.

Air Fryer Cheese Stuffed Mushrooms

Ingredients:

- 8 oz fresh mushrooms
- 4 oz cream cheese
- ¼ Cup shredded parmesan cheese
- 1/8 cup shredded sharp cheddar cheese
- 1/8 cup shredded white cheddar cheese
- 1 teaspoon Worcestershire sauce
- 2 garlic cloves Minced
- Salt and pepper to taste

Directions:

1. Cut the stem out of the mushroom to prepare it for stuffing. I first chop off the stem, and then make a circular cut around the area where the stem was. Continue to cut until you have removed excess mushroom.
2. Place the cream cheese in the microwave for 15 seconds to soften.
3. Combine the cream cheese, all of the shredded cheeses, salt, pepper, garlic, and Worcestershire sauce in a medium bowl. Stir to combine.
4. Stuff the mushrooms with the cheese mixture.
5. Place the mushrooms in the Air Fryer for 8 minutes on 370 degrees.
6. Allow the mushrooms to cool before serving.

Air Fryer Zucchini Fries

Ingredients:

- 2 medium zucchini
- 1 large egg beaten
- ½ cup almond flour or panko/Italian breadcrumbs
- ½ Cup parmesan cheese grated
- 1 teaspoon Italian seasoning or seasoning of choice
- ½ Teaspoon garlic powder optional
- Pinch of salt and pepper
- Oil for spraying olive or oil of choice

Directions:

1. Cut the zucchini in half and into sticks (aka fries) about 1/2 inch thick and 3-4 inches long.
2. In a shallow bowl, combine the almond flour (or bread crumbs), grated parmesan, spices and a pinch of salt and pepper. Mix to combine.
3. Dredge zucchini in egg and then in the almond flour mixture and place on a plate or baking sheet. Generously spray zucchini with cooking spray.
4. Working in batches, place the zucchini fries in a single layer in the air fryer. And Cook for 10 minutes at 400F, or until crispy.

Keto Air Fryer Mozzarella Sticks

Servings: 4   **Cook Time: 8 Mins**   **Prep Time: 15 Mins**

Ingredients:

- 6 mozzarella string cheese sticks (MUST be low moisture, part skim)
- 1-2 large eggs, beaten
- 1/2 cup finely grated parmesan cheese
- 1/3 cup almond flour
- 1 teaspoon Italian seasoning
- 1/2 teaspoon garlic powder
- 1/4 teaspoon sea salt

Directions:

1. If needed, prep your air fryer basket insert with a tin foil liner.
2. Unwrap the cheese sticks and cut in half to create two shorter sticks from each. Set aside.
3. Beat your egg/eggs in a small to medium bowl. You can start with one egg and add another later if needed.
4. In a medium dish (large enough to make it easy to coat your cheese sticks) blend together the parmesan cheese, almond flour, Italian seasoning, garlic powder, and sea salt.
5. Create a dipping station starting with your (previously cut) cheese sticks, followed by the egg wash, then the "breading" mix, and finally a small pan or dish covered with a sheet of parchment paper.
6. One by one, dip each cheese stick in the egg wash followed by rolling the cheese stick in the "breading" mix. I use a method to help adhere the "breading" to the cheese by rolling between my palms which helps to press and secure the almond flour/parmesan coating onto the cheese stick. Repeat these steps a second time before placing the fully coated cheese stick on the parchment paper. To summarize, be sure that each cheese stick gets two egg washes and two rolls in the almond flour/parmesan breading.
7. Once all the cheese sticks have been dipped and rolled, check each one to make sure that no cheese is showing through. Re-roll any that need extra "breading". If the cheese stick isn't fully coated, there is a greater risk that cheese will ooze out during cooking. You should have very little of the almond flour/parmesan mixture left by the time you are done with the coating process. Feel free to use it up by re-rolling any that look like they need a little extra lovin'.
8. Place the pan/dish with cheese sticks in the freezer on a level surface for no less than 1 hour. This helps to keep the cheese from melting too quickly in the high heat of the air fryer giving the outer coating time to get crispy.
9. Once frozen through, remove the cheese sticks from the freezer. With cooking spray, grease your air fryer basket and/or tin foil liner AS WELL AS each cheese stick. (I spray the top side then roll them over and spray the other side.)
10. Place cheese sticks in an air fryer. (If you have a smaller air fryer, you may want to separate into two batches as the mozzarella sticks puff a bit while cooking.) Cook at 375 degrees (or 380 if your Air Fryer doesn't have 5 degree increments) for 7-10 minutes depending on your air fryer.
11. I set my Philips turbostar to 375 degrees and cook them for about 8 minutes. After 5 minutes in the air fryer, I

suggest checking them every minute or so moving forward. If you see the cheese start to ooze out, then it's time to pull them.

12. Serve immediately to ensure that your fried mozzarella sticks remain crispy, melty, and gooey. I like to accompany mine with no-sugar-added marinara and ranch dressing. Enjoy!

Air Fryer Mexican Street Corn Recipe

Servings: 4   **Cook Time: 15 Mins**   **Prep Time: 15 Mins**

Ingredients:

- 4 pieces fresh corn on the cob cleaned
- 1/4 cup crumbled cotija cheese or Feta cheese
- 1/4 teaspoon chili powder
- 1/2 teaspoon Stone House Seasoning
- 1/4 cup chopped fresh cilantro
- 1 medium lime cut into wedges

Directions:

1. Place corn into the air fryer basket and cook at 390°F for 10 minutes.
2. Sprinkle corn with cheese and cook at 390°F for 5 more minutes.
3. Remove from air fryer and sprinkle with chili powder, Stone House Seasoning, and cilantro. Serve with lime wedges.

Killer Garlic Fries with Rosemary

Servings: 8   Cook Time: 25 Mins   Prep Time: 5 Mins

Ingredients:

- 1 28 ounce bag Alexia House Cut Fries with Sea Salt
- 1/3 cup canola oil
- 1/4 cup pressed garlic
- 1 tablespoon minced fresh rosemary
- 1 tablespoon minced parsley
- 1 teaspoon kosher salt
- 1/2 teaspoon freshly ground black pepper

Directions:

1. Preheat the oven to 400°F.
2. Spread the fries evenly on a baking sheet and bake for 15-20 minutes or until crisp, stirring halfway during cooking.
3. While the fries are baking, mix the canola oil with the garlic and rosemary and 1/2 teaspoon of the kosher salt. (This step can be done ahead of time.)
4. Remove the fries from the oven and transfer to a large bowl with the garlic, rosemary and oil mixture and season with the remaining kosher salt and ground pepper. Toss well with tongs until combined and serve immediately.

Notes

5. To make in an air fryer: Cook the fries in the air fryer at 400°F for 15-20 minutes, then toss with the garlic and oil mixture as directed above.

Low Carb Keto Air Fryer Radish Chips

Servings: 2   **Cook Time: 18 Mins**   **Prep Time: 2 Mins**

Ingredients:

- One bag of radish slices
- Avocado oil or olive oil in a spritzer
- salt
- pepper
- garlic powder
- onion powder

Directions:

1. Wash and pat dry radish slices. Place radishes in air fryer basket and spread out evenly. Spritz 3-4 times with oil. Sprinkle with salt, pepper, garlic powder, and onion powder.
2. Cook in air fryer for 5 minutes at 370°. Give them a little stir and cook another 5 minutes.
3. Spritz 3-4 more times with oil after 10 minutes and sprinkle with a little more salt, pepper, garlic powder, and onion powder.
4. Cook another 5 minutes and give them another stir. Cook another 3 more minutes keeping a close eye that they don't get too crispy.

Low Carb Air Fryer Pickles

Ingredients:

- 1 large egg
- 3/4 cup heavy cream
- 1/4 tsp cayenne pepper
- 2 oz (4 cups) pork rinds
- 1/2 cup almond flour
- 2 tbsps freeze dried dill
- 2 tsps paprika
- 2 tsps black pepper
- 35 dill pickle slices
- Sriracha Mayo (Lee Kum Kee brand is my favorite)
- Ranch dressing

Directions:

1. In a small bowl beat together egg, heavy cream and cayenne.
2. Add pork rinds to the bowl of a food processor and process until they resemble crumbs. Place 1/2 cup of the pork rinds in a shallow bowl. In another bowl, mix the rest of the pork rinds with almond flour, dill, paprika and black pepper.
3. Dip each pickle slice in the plain pork rinds, then the egg wash, then the almond flour mixture until all are coated.
4. Working in batches, air fry pickle slices in a single layer at 390 degrees F for 8-10 minutes or until golden brown.
5. Serve immediately with Sriracha Mayo and Ranch dressing for dipping.

Air Fryer Chicken

Chicken Parmesan In The Air Fryer

Servings: 4   **Cook Time: 10 Mins**   **Prep Time: 15 Mins**

Ingredients:

- 2 8 ounce boneless skinless chicken breasts, sliced lengthwise to make 4 thinner cutlets
- 6 tbsp seasoned breadcrumbs, whole wheat or gluten-free
- 2 tbsp grated Parmesan cheese
- 1 tbsp butter, melted (or olive oil)
- 6 tbsp reduced fat mozzarella cheese, I used Polly-o
- 1/2 cup marinara
- olive oil spray

Directions:

1. Combine breadcrumbs and parmesan cheese in a bowl. Melt the butter in another bowl.
2. Lightly brush the butter onto the chicken, then dip into breadcrumb mixture.
3. When the air fryer is ready, transfer to the air fryer basket, in batches as needed and spray the top with oil.
4. Air fryer 360F° 5 minutes, turn and top each with 2 tbsp sauce and 1 1/2 tbsp of shredded mozzarella cheese.
5. Cook 3 more minutes or until cheese is melted.

Air Fryer Chicken Nuggets Recipe

Ingredients:

- 1 boneless skinless chicken breast
- 1/4 teaspoon salt
- 1/8 teaspoon black pepper
- 1/2 cup unsalted butter melted
- 1/2 cup breadcrumbs
- 2 tablespoons grated Parmesan optional

Directions:

1. Preheat air fryer to 390 degrees for 4 minutes.
2. Trim any fat from chicken breast, Slice into 1/2 inch thick slices, then each slice into 2 to 3 nuggets. Season chicken pieces with salt and pepper.
3. Place melted butter in a small bowl and breadcrumbs (with Parmesan, if using) in another small bowl.
4. Dip each piece of chicken in butter, then breadcrumbs.
5. Place in a single layer in the air fryer basket. Depending on the size of your air fryer, you may need to bake in two batches or more.
6. Set timer to 8 minutes.
7. When done, check if the internal temperature of chicken nuggets is at least 165 degrees F. Remove nuggets from basket with tongs and set onto a plate to cool.

NOTES

Serve with steamed or roasted vegetables or fruit salad and yogurt.

This recipe makes about 21 chicken nuggets from one chicken breast. You can double and use two chicken breast and make 42 nuggets, which is comparable to the amount you get in a bag in a grocery store.

You can use plain breadcrumbs, however I prefer Italian style.

The amount of calories does not include Parmesan cheese, which is optional.

Low Carb Keto Fried Chicken In An Air Fryer Or Oven

Ingredients:

- 5 pounds chicken about 10 pieces
- 1 cup almond milk
- 1 tablespoon white vinegar
- 2 cups crushed pork rinds
- 1/2 teaspoon salt
- 1/2 teaspoon thyme
- 1/3 teaspoon oregano
- 1/2 teaspoon basil
- 1 teaspoon celery salt
- 1 teaspoon black pepper
- 4 teaspoons paprika
- 1 teaspoon dried mustard
- 2 teaspoons garlic salt
- 1 teaspoon ground ginger
- 3 teaspoons white pepper
- 1 tablespoon coconut oil for air fryer only

Directions:

1. Place chicken in a large bowl. Mix almond milk and vinegar then pour over chicken. Let the chicken soak in the liquid for 2 hours in the refrigerator.
2. In wide shallow bowl or dish, combine pork rinds, salt, thyme, basil, oregano, celery salt, black pepper, dried mustard, paprika, garlic salt, ground ginger, and white pepper.
3. Dip each piece of chicken in dry pork rind mixture until coated.
4. Air fryer:
5. Spread 1 tablespoon coconut oil in bottom of air fryer basket.
6. Arrange chicken in single layer on basket.
7. Air fry at 360°F for 10 minutes, rotate, then air fry another 10 minutes. Test chicken temperature to reach 165°F and continue cooking if needed.
8. Oven:
9. Arrange chicken on a rack in baking pan. Bake at 350°F for about 50 minutes or until meat reaches 165°F.

Herb-Marinated Air Fryer Chicken Thighs

Servings: 8   **Cook Time: 35 Mins**   **Prep Time: 15 Mins**

Ingredients:

- 8 bone-in, skin-on chicken thighs
- 1/4 cup olive oil
- 2 T lemon juice
- 2 tsp. Garlic powder
- 1 tsp. Spike seasoning, or use any all-purpose herb blend.

- 1 tsp. Dried basil
- 1/2 tsp. Dried oregano
- 1/2 tsp. Onion powder
- 1/2 tsp. Dried sage
- 1/4 tsp. Black pepper

Directions:

1. Trim some of the skin and most of the fat from the chicken thighs. (I used kitchen shears to trim the chicken.) I like to make short slits through the skin and into the meat, but that's not essential.

2. Mix together olive oil, lemon juice, garlic powder, Spike Seasoning or another seasoning blend, dried basil, dried oregano, onion powder, dried sage, and black pepper to make the marinade.

3. Put chicken thighs in a Ziploc bag or plastic container with a snap-tight lid, add the marinade and let the chicken marinate in the fridge at least 6 hours, or all day while you're at work.

4. When it's time to cook, drain the chicken well in a colander placed in the sink and discard marinade.

5. Arrange chicken top-side down in the air fryer basket or on a baking rack and let the chicken come to room temperature while you preheat the air fryer to 360F/185C (if needed) or preheat the oven to 400F/200C.

6. TO COOK IN AIR FRYER: Cook chicken top-side down in the pre-heated air fryer for 8 minutes. Then turn the chicken thighs over and cook about 6 minutes more. After six minutes, check the chicken to see if some pieces are getting too browned and rearrange the chicken thighs in the air-fryer basket if needed. (I switched some of the outside more-browned pieces to the inside and I think some pieces would have burned if I hadn't done that.) Cook about 6 minutes more, or until the chicken is well-browned with crispy skin and the internal temperature is at least 165F/75C.

7. TO COOK IN THE OVEN: If you have a baking rack that lets hot air flow around the chicken, use that on top of your baking sheet. Cook chicken top-side down in the preheated oven for 10 minutes. Then turn chicken pieces over and cook about 25 minutes longer, or until the chicken is well-browned, skin is crisp, and the internal temperature is at least 165F/75C.

8. No matter which cooking method you use, I recommend using an Instant-Read Meat Thermometer to check the internal temperature of the chicken if you have one.

9. Serve hot. If you want to use the air fryer and need to cook two batches for a larger family, keep the first batch warm in a 200F/100C oven while the second batch cooks.

Crispy Parmesan Buttermilk Chicken Tenders

Servings: 4   **Cook Time: 18 Mins**   **Prep Time: 10 Mins**

Ingredients:

- 2 boneless skinless chicken breasts
- 3/4 cup buttermilk
- 1 1/2 teaspoons Worcestershire sauce , divided
- 3/4 teaspoon kosher salt , divided
- 3/4 teaspoon freshly ground black pepper , divided
- 1/2 teaspoon smoked paprika , divided
- 2 tablespoons butter
- 1 1/2 cups panko breadcrumbs
- 1/4 cup ground Parmesan cheese
- 2 large eggs
- 1/2 cup all-purpose flour
- Honey mustard sauce, barbecue sauce, or Ranch dressing , for dipping

Directions:

1. Use a chef's knife to trim the fat from the chicken breasts and cut into tenders, about 5 per breast. Tap the thicker parts of the tenders with the flat part of the knife to even the thickness, about 1/2 inch at most.
2. In a bowl or jar with a fitted lid, combine the buttermilk with half of the Worcestershire sauce, and half of the salt and pepper and paprika. Add to a gallon freezer bag with the chicken and refrigerate for at least 6 hours or up to overnight.
3. Melt the butter in a small saucepan over medium heat, watching closely as the butter melts and begins to foam and changes to a golden color with a nutty aroma. Remove the browned butter from the heat and let cook slightly.
4. Combine the panko and the butter on a plate, tossing until well combined, then add the Parmesan cheese and toss. In a shallow bowl, whisk the eggs with the remaining Worcestershire sauce. On another plate, toss the flour with the remaining salt, pepper and smoked paprika.
5. Drain the chicken and discard the buttermilk. Using tongs, work with one tender at a time and dredge the chicken through the flour to coat, then the egg, and then the panko.

To Bake:

6. Position an oven rack in the upper third of the oven and preheat the oven to 375°F. Lightly brush a wire rack with oil and place it on a rimmed baking sheet.
7. Place the crumb-coated chicken on the prepared rack. Repeat with the remaining chicken. Bake for 18-20 minutes or until the panko is pale golden and the chicken is cooked through. Finish the chicken under the broiler for a crispier, more browned coating.

To Air Fry:

8. Preheat the air fryer to 400°F. Place the chicken tenders in the basket, adding in batches so not to crowd or overlap.
9. Cook for 13-15 minutes, flipping the chicken half way through so they're crispy on both sides. Repeat with the remaining tenders.
10. Serve with sauces.

Notes

While this recipe is terrific for an easy dinner, it's smart to make a double batch while you're cooking, to use through the week for lunchtime salads, wraps, and over meal prepped grains with roasted vegetables or roasted broccoli.

Chicken tenders can be refrigerated for 3 days. Freeze for up to 2 months and reheat from frozen for 20-25 min at 350°F.

Air Fryer Whole Roast Chicken

Servings: 4-6   **Cook Time: 1 hour**   **Prep Time: 5 Mins**

Ingredients:

- 1 whole chicken (up to 2kg, depending on the size of your air fryer)
- 1tbsp olive oil
- 1tsp smoked paprika
- 1tsp dried mixed herbs
- 1tsp garlic granules/salt

Directions:

1. Using a brush, coat the chicken in olive oil.
2. Mix the seasoning together and paste it all over the chicken. Make up some more spice mix if there isn't enough to coat the whole chicken.
3. Place the chicken in the air fryer basket, breast side down. Cook at 180°C for 45 minutes. Check on it once or twice to ensure it is cooking ok and not burning.
4. At 45 minutes, turn the chicken over so that it is breast side up. Cook for a further 15 minutes.
5. Check the chicken has cooked through. You can pierce it with a sharp knife to see if the juices run clear - or, my preferred way, use a meat thermometer to check the internal temperature. If it isn't cooked through, return it to the air fryer and cook for some more time, checking on it every so often.

Notes

Serve with chips, potato wedges, rice, salad - anything goes with chicken.

Experiment with different seasoning rubs, and you can change up the taste each time.

Air Fryer Chicken Wings

Servings: 4   Cook Time: 25 Mins   Prep Time: 5 Mins

Ingredients:

- 1 kg chicken wings
- 1 tbsp olive oil
- ½ tsp garlic powder
- ½ tsp onion powder
- ½ tsp paprika
- ½ tsp salt
- ½ tsp black pepper

Directions:

1. Preheat the air fryer at 180C.
2. Prepare the chicken wings by firstly patting them dry with some kitchen roll. The dryer the chicken wings are, the crispier they will come out.
3. Add the wings to a large bowl and cover with the olive oil, tossing them so that they are all covered as much as possible.
4. Add all the seasonings, coating all the wings.
5. Put the chicken wings in the air fryer. Depending on how many wings you are cooking, and the size of your air fryer, you might need to do them in batches. You can also use a rack in your air fryer to fit more in. The key thing is to make sure the wings are not touching each other so that they have room to crisp up.
6. Cook for 20 minutes, turning and shaking 2 or 3 times to ensure they cook evenly.
7. Increase the temperature to 200C and cook for a further 5 minutes or until the skin is crispy.
8. Serve with BBQ sauce, Hot Pepper Sauce, Buffalo Sauce

Crispy Keto Chicken Nugget Recipe In The Air Fryer

Servings: 28 **Cook Time: 20 Mins** **Prep Time: 5 Mins**

Ingredients:

- 1 lb chicken tenders
- 1 bag pork rinds (3.25 oz)
- 1/2 cup parmesan cheese
- 1 teaspoon paprika
- 1 teaspoon garlic powder
- 1/4 cup mayo
- 1 teaspoon onion powder

Directions:

1. Spray the basket of the air fryer with cooking oil.
2. Pour the contents of the pork rinds in to a baggie and crush or add to a food processor and grind until they form bread crumbs. Pour into a large shallow bowl and mix in the spices and cheese.
3. Either cut the tenders in to small bite sized pieces or just add the tenders as is to a large plastic baggie and spoon the mayo on top.
4. Squish the mayo and chicken around to cover the chicken completely. Note you can also add the mayo to a separate bowl and coat them that way. The baggie just seems easier to me.
5. Take a piece of chicken and roll around in the shallow bowl of bread crumbs and then carefully place in the basket of the air fryer. Continue with all of the chicken pieces.
6. Cook for 10-15 minutes at 380° F and then 3-5 minutes. At 400°F. Check to make sure the chicken is cooked, especially with the tenders. They should be golden brown and an internal temperature of 165° F.
7. Serve immediately.

Air Fryer Buffalo Chicken Hot Wings

Servings: 5   Cook Time: 29 Mins   Prep Time: 5 Mins

Ingredients:

Wings:

- 2 pounds chicken wingettes
- 1 tablespoon olive oil or avocado oil
- 1/2 teaspoon garlic powder
- 1/2 teaspoon salt
- Extra oil for greasing

Buffalo sauce:

- 1/3 cup hot pepper sauce I used Frank's Red Hot
- 1/4 cup butter or butter flavored coconut oil for dairy-free
- 1 tablespoon white vinegar
- 1/8 teaspoon ground chipolte pepper or cayenne pepper

Directions:

Wings:

1. In large bowl, rub olive oil on chicken wings and then sprinkle on the garlic powder and salt.
2. Rub inside of air fryer basket with a little more olive oil, avocado oil, or coconut oil.
3. Place chicken wings in a single layer in basket.
4. Cook wings at 360°F for 25 minutes.
5. Flip wings over. Then increase temperature to 400°F and cook for 4 more minutes.

Sauce:

6. While wings are cooking in air fryer, combine hot sauce, butter, vinegar, and ground pepper in small pot.
7. Bring sauce to a boil on medium heat while whisking everything together. Remove from heat and set aside.
8. When wings are done, add them to the sauce and coat each piece evenly.
9. Serve with blue cheese dressing and celery.

Keto Fried Chicken Tenders Chick-Fil-A Copycat Recipe

Servings: 8   **Cook Time: 15 Mins**   **Prep Time: 10 Mins**

Ingredients:

- Keto fried chicken tenders
- 8 chicken tenders
- 24oz Jar of Dill Pickles (you only need the juice)
- 3/4 cup now foods almond flour
- 1 tsp Salt
- 1 tsp Pepper
- 2 Eggs, beaten
- 1 1/2 Cups pork panko (Bread Crumb Substitute)
- Nutiva Organic Coconut Oil for frying
- Low carb copycat chick-fil-a sauce
- 1/2 cup mayo
- 2 tsp Yellow Mustard
- 1 tsp Lemon Juice
- 2 tbs Honey Trees Sugar-Free Honey
- 1 tbs Primal Kitchen Classic BBQ Sauce

Directions:

1. Pan fried keto chicken tenders
2. Put chicken tenders and pickle juice in a large zip lock bag and marinate for at least 1 hour, preferably overnight.
3. In a small bowl, mix almond flour, salt, and pepper
4. Create an assembly line of three bowls, one with almond flour mixture, the second with the eggs and the third with the pork panko
5. Dredge the Chicken in the almond flour mixture, then in the egg and finally in the pork panko until well coated
6. Now, fill a saute pan about 2 inches with coconut oil and put on medium-high heat. If available use a thermometer and bring oil to 350 F
7. Once the oil is hot place tenders in the oil and cook about 3 minutes on each side or until golden brown.
8. Air fryer fried keto chicken tenders
9. Put chicken tenders and pickle juice in a large zip lock bag and marinate for at least 1 hour, preferably overnight.
10. In a small bowl, mix almond flour, salt, and pepper
11. Create an assembly line of three bowls, one with almond flour mixture, the second with the eggs and the third with the pork panko
12. Dredge the Chicken in the almond flour mixture, then in the egg and finally in the pork panko until well coated
13. Set the air fryer to 375 F and cook the chicken for about 15 minutes.
14. Low carb copycat chick-fil-a sauce
15. In a small bowl, combine all ingredients and stir until fully combined

Air Fryer Sesame Chicken Breast

Ingredients:

- 2 chicken breasts (skin-on, boneless or bone-in)
- 2 Tbsp sesame oil
- 1 tsp kosher salt (plus more to taste)
- 1/2 tsp black pepper
- 1 Tbsp sweet paprika
- 1/4 tsp cayenne pepper (optional)
- 1 Tbsp granulated garlic (or garlic powder)
- 1 Tbsp granulated onions (or onion powder)

Directions:

1. Rub the chicken breasts with sesame oil. Sprinkle salt, pepper and the rest of ingredients all over. Pat down and rub gently to ensure even coverage.
2. Place chicken breasts on the rack inside the air fryer, ensuring some space between the chicken breasts, skin side up.
3. Plug in your air fryer, set the temperature to 380F and the time to 20 minutes. When the 20 minutes of cooking is up, flip the breasts and continue cooking for another 10 minutes.
4. Remove chicken breasts from the air fryer and set on a plate. Let rest for 5 minutes, then serve.

Air Fryer Lemon Pepper Chicken Wings

Ingredients:

- 1.5 lbs to 2 lbs. Chicken wings, separated and wing tips discarded
- 1 tbsp Lemon Pepper seasoning

Directions:

1. Preheat your air fryer to 380 degrees F for 5 minutes.
2. Toss the chicken wings with the seasoning and place the wings in the basket of your air fryer in an even layer. Cook at 380 degrees F for 10 minutes, flip the wings and cook an additional 10 minutes.
3. Serve wings with your favorite dipping sauce. Enjoy!

Air Fryer Keto Popcorn Chicken

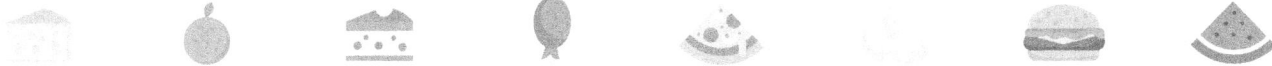

Servings: 6 **Cook Time: 10 Mins** **Prep Time: 15 Mins**

Ingredients:

- 1.5 lb chicken breasts
- 1/4 cup coconut flour
- 1/2 tsp sea salt
- 1/4 tsp ground black pepper
- 4 eggs
- 2 1/2 cups pork panko
- 1 tsp onion powder
- 1 tsp garlic powder
- 1 tsp paprika

Directions:

1. In a small bowl, combine coconut flour, sea salt, and ground black pepper.
2. In another bowl, crack the eggs and whisk them together.
3. In the 3rd bowl, mix together pork panko, onion powder, garlic powder, and paprika.
4. Cut the chicken into bite-sized pieces, and transfer to a large mixing bowl.
5. Sprinkle the coconut flour mixture over the chicken and toss together gently until all of the chicken is covered evenly.
6. Working in batches, dredge the chicken pieces in the egg wash.
7. Shake off the excess and press into the pork panko mixture. Transfer to a plate and repeat with the rest of the chicken.
8. Air fryer method
9. Lightly grease the air fryer basket, then preheat the air fryer to 400 degrees F for about 5 minutes.
10. Add the chicken into the air fryer basket in an even layer. If you have a small air fryer, you may need to split it up into 2 batches.
11. Cook for 10-12 minutes in the air fryer, shaking halfway through.
12. If you'd like, enjoy dipped in Whole30 "honey" mustard!
13. Oven method
14. Preheat the oven to 400 degrees F and line a baking sheet with a wire rack.
15. Place the chicken pieces on the wire rack without touching each other.
16. Bake for 15 minutes until crispy and golden.
17. If you'd like, enjoy dipped in Whole30 "honey" mustard!

Air Fryer Chicken Fajitas

Ingredients:

- 2 chicken breasts boneless and skinless, cut into strips (around 1 pound/450g)
- 1 red bell pepper sliced into ½ inch slices
- 1 yellow bell pepper sliced into ½ inch slices
- 1 green bell pepper sliced into ½ inch slices
- 1 red onion sliced into wedges
- 3 tablespoons fajita seasoning
- 1 tablespoon vegetable oil

Directions:

1. Preheat the Air Fryer to 390°F (200°C).
2. Drizzle oil over the chicken strips, and season with the fajita seasoning. Toss well and make sure that they're evenly coated with the seasoning. Add the veggies, and season well. Make sure that everything is well coated in fajita seasoning.
3. Put everything in an Air Fryer basket. Air Fry at for 15 minutes, tossing halfway through.
4. Serve with warmed tortillas, pico de gallo, avocado slices or guacamole.

Air Fryer Chicken Tenders

Servings: 2   **Cook Time: 10 Mins**   **Prep Time: 8 Mins**

Ingredients:

- 1–1/2 lbs. Chicken tenders
- 2 eggs
- 1 cup fine almond flour
- 2 tablespoon ground flax seed
- 1 teaspoon Italian seasoning
- 1 teaspoon fine sea salt
- 1 teaspoon paprika
- 1/2 teaspoon ground black pepper
- 1/2 teaspoon garlic powder
- 1/2 teaspoon onion powder
- Avocado oil spray

Directions:

1. Pre-heat air fryer to 400°f.
2. Pat chicken dry with paper towel and season with a pinch of salt and pepper.
3. In a medium bowl whisk eggs.
4. In a wide shallow container, whisk almond flour, flaxseed, and all of the seasoning, until combined.
5. Dip sliced chicken into the egg, then dredge in flour mixture. Repeat until all chicken is coated.
6. Spray the air fryer basket generously with avocado spray, and place as many chicken tenders in the basket that will fit with plenty of space in between. Spray tenders with additional avocado spray to lightly coat.
7. Fry for 10 minutes, flipping once at 5 minutes.
8. Repeat with remaining chicken tenders until they have all been cooked through to reach an internal temperature of 165°f.
9. Serve with your favorite dipping sauce.

Air Fryer Chicken Wings Recipe

Servings: 4   **Cook Time: 35 Mins**   **Prep Time: 5 Mins**

Ingredients:

- 2 lb Chicken wings (flats and drumettes, either fresh or thawed from frozen)
- 2 tsp Baking powder
- 3/4 tsp Sea salt
- 1/4 tsp Black pepper

Directions:

1. Pat the chicken wings very dry with paper towels. (This will help them get crispy.)
2. In a large bowl, toss the wings with baking powder, sea salt and black pepper.
3. Place the chicken wings in the air fryer in a single layer, without touching too much. (Cook in batches if they don't fit.)
4. Air fry the chicken wings for 15 minutes at 250 degrees F. (If your wings are frozen, add an extra 10 minutes at this step.)
5. Flip the wings over. Increase the air fryer temperature to 430 degrees F (or the highest your air fryer goes). Air fry for about 15 to 20 minutes, until chicken wings are done and crispy.

Easy, Air Fryer Grilled Chicken Kebabs

Servings: 4   **Cook Time: 20 Mins**   **Prep Time: 15 Mins**

Ingredients:

- 16 oz skinless chicken breasts, cut into 1-inch cubes
- 2 tablespoons soy sauce or liquid aminos (keto and gluten-free)
- 1 tablespoon mccormick's Grill Mates Chicken Seasoning
- 1 teaspoon mccormick's Grill Mates BBQ Seasoning
- Salt and pepper to taste
- ½ Green pepper sliced
- ½ Red pepper sliced
- ½ Yellow pepper sliced
- ½ Zucchini sliced
- ¼ Red onion sliced
- 4-5 grape tomatoes
- Cooking oil spray optional

Directions:

1. Marinating the chicken is preferred but not required. If you plan to marinate the chicken, place the chicken in a sealable plastic bag or large bowl with the soy sauce, chicken seasoning, BBQ seasoning, and salt and pepper to taste. Shake the bag to ensure the chicken is evenly coated and seasoning. If using a bowl, cover the bowl. Marinate for at least one hour to overnight in the refrigerator.
2. Remove the chicken and thread it onto a skewer. Your hands will get very messy during this process. You may want to have a towel close by to wipe your hands.
3. Layer the chicken with the peppers, zucchini, and onions. Top each skewer with a grape tomato at the top. I sometimes like my grape tomato to be served cooked and soft. It may be harder to get the skewers to fit into your air fryer with the tomato (depending on the brand). You can always add the tomato after the chicken and veggies have finished cooking.
4. Spray the chicken and veggies with cooking oil (I use olive oil). This is optional and yields juicy chicken.
5. I like to line the air fryer with parchment paper liners for easy clean up.
6. Place the skewers on a grill rack in the air fryer basket. Cook for 10 minutes on 350 degrees.
7. Open the air fryer and flip the skewers. Cook for an additional 7-10 minutes until the chicken reaches an internal temperature of 165 degrees. Use a meat thermometer to test the inside of one of the pieces of chicken.

Air Fryer Chicken Fajitas

Servings: 4

Servings: 4　　**Cook Time: 15 Mins**　　**Prep Time: 5 Mins**

Ingredients:

- 6 boneless chicken thighs (or 4 chicken breasts)
- 1 onion, chopped
- 3 sweet peppers, deseeded and sliced
- 2 tbsp fajita spice mix*
- 1 tbsp olive oil
- 1 tbsp chipotle paste **
- Juice of half a lime

Directions:

1. Slice the chicken into strips.
2. Mix the oil, fajita spice, chipotle paste, and lime juice in a bowl.
3. Add the chicken strips to the bowl and leave to marinate for at least ten minutes.
4. While the chicken is marinating, prepare the onions and peppers by chopping them into equal-sized pieces.
5. Preheat the air fryer to 200C/390F.
6. Transfer the chicken to the air fryer basket and air fry for 10 minutes, shaking halfway through.
7. Add the vegetables and stir through. Close the air fryer and cook for a further 5 minutes.
8. Transfer to a bowl and serve in a tortilla wrap with salsa and guacamole.

Notes

*Fajita Spice Mix

If you don't have a fajita spice mix you can make up your own. Try mixing the following together;

- 2 tsp ground cumin
- 2 tsp smoked paprika
- 2 tsp ground oregano
- 1 tsp chilli powder

**Chipotle Paste

This is optional but it adds an extra kick to the fajitas flavour

Air Fryer Piri Piri Chicken Legs

Servings: 4 **Cook Time: 22 Mins** **Prep Time: 5 Mins**

Ingredients:

- 4 chicken legs
- 2 tsp Piri Piri spice mix
- 120g Piri Piri marinade sauce (approx)

Directions:

1. Add the spice mix and sauce to the raw chicken legs. Leave them to marinate for around 30 minutes.
2. Transfer to the air fryer basket and cook at 190°C/375°F for 22 minutes.
3. Turn the chicken legs at the halfway mark.
4. The chicken legs are ready when the juices run clear and the internal temperature is 75°C/165°F – use a meat thermometer if necessary.

Buffalo Chicken Air Fryer Chicken Legs

Servings: 2 **Cook Time: 25 Mins** **Prep Time: 5 Mins**

Ingredients:

- 2 Lbs Chicken Drumsticks, (skin removed)
- 2 Tablespoons Ghee, (melted)
- 1/4 Cup Frank's redhot Original Sauce

Directions:

1. Spray air fryer basket with nonstick oil. Preheat air fryer at 400° for 2-3 minutes.
2. Place drumsticks in basket, air fry at 400° for 15 minutes.
3. Flip drumsticks and air fry at 400° for 5 more minutes.
4. Mix melted ghee and hot sauce in large bowl. Transfer drumsticks to bowl and toss in sauce. Return drumsticks to basket and spoon remaining sauce over the top of the drumsticks. Air fry for 5 more minutes or until internal chicken temp reaches 165°f.
5. Serve with Whole30 Ranch Dip, celery and carrots.

Air Fryer Whole Roast Chicken

Servings: 4-6 **Cook Time: 1 hour** **Prep Time: 5 Mins**

Ingredients:

- 1 whole chicken (up to 2kg, depending on the size of your air fryer)
- 1tbsp olive oil
- 1tsp smoked paprika
- 1tsp dried mixed herbs
- 1tsp garlic granules/salt

Directions:

1. Using a brush, coat the chicken in olive oil.
2. Mix the seasoning together and paste it all over the chicken. Make up some more spice mix if there isn't enough to coat the whole chicken.
3. Place the chicken in the air fryer basket, breast side down. Cook at 180°C for 45 minutes. Check on it once or twice to ensure it is cooking ok and not burning.
4. At 45 minutes, turn the chicken over so that it is breast side up. Cook for a further 15 minutes.
5. Check the chicken has cooked through. You can pierce it with a sharp knife to see if the juices run clear - or, my preferred way, use a meat thermometer to check the internal temperature. If it isn't cooked through, return it to the air fryer and cook for some more time, checking on it every so often.

Notes

Serve with chips, potato wedges, rice, salad - anything goes with chicken.

Experiment with different seasoning rubs, and you can change up the taste each time.

Air Fryer Chicken Breasts

Servings: 4   **Cook Time: 20 Mins**   **Prep Time: 10 Mins**

Ingredients:

- 1 chicken breast (increase accordingly)
- 1/2 tbsp olive oil
- 1/2 tsp salt
- 1/2 tsp pepper
- 1/2 tsp garlic powder (or seasoning of your choice)

Directions:

1. Preheat the air fryer at 180°C (360°F).
2. Brush or spray each chicken breast with oil.
3. Season one side (the smooth side) of each chicken breast.
4. Place each chicken breast (smooth side down) in the air fryer basket. Season the other side.
5. Set the timer for 10 minutes.
6. After 10 minutes turn the chicken breasts over to allow them to cook on both sides.
7. Check the chicken is cooked all the way through - use a meat thermometer if necessary.
8. Leave the chicken to rest for 5 minutes before serving or slicing.

Notes

Cooking Times

Cooking times will vary depending on your air fryer and the size of the chicken breasts. Use the following times as a guide:

150g - 200g: 16 to 18 minutes

200g - 300g: 18 to 20 minutes

Always check the chicken is cooked all the way through (the juices should run clear and there should be no pink bits).

Air Fryer Keto Low Carb Fried Chicken Recipe

Servings: 6   **Cook Time: 20 Mins**   **Prep Time: 10 Mins**

Ingredients:

- 2 1/2 lbs Chicken drumsticks
- 1/4 cup Wholesome Yum Coconut Flour
- 1/2 tsp Sea salt
- 1/4 tsp Black pepper
- 2 large Eggs
- 1 cup Pork rinds (2.25 oz)
- 1 tsp Smoked paprika
- 1/2 tsp Garlic powder
- 1/4 tsp Dried thyme

Directions:

1. Stir the coconut flour, sea salt and black pepper in a medium shallow bowl. Set aside.
2. In a second medium bowl, whisk together the eggs. Set aside.
3. In a third bowl, mix the crushed pork rinds, smoked paprika, garlic powder and thyme.
4. Dredge the chicken pieces in the coconut flour mixture, dip in the eggs, shake off the excess, then press into the pork rind mixture. For best results, keep most of the third mixture in a separate bowl and add a little at a time to the bowl where you'll be coating the chicken. That way, it won't get clumpy too fast.
5. Preheat the air fryer at 400 degrees F (204 degrees C) for 5 minutes. Lightly grease the metal basket and arrange the breaded chicken on it in a single layer, without touching.
6. Place the basket into the air fryer. Cook the fried chicken in the air fryer for 20 minutes, until it reaches an internal temperature of 165 degrees F (74 degrees C).

Low Carb Keto Paleo Baked Chicken Nuggets In The Air Fryer

Servings: 4   **Cook Time: 15 Mins**   **Prep Time: 10 Mins**

Ingredients:

- 1 Pound Free-range boneless, skinless chicken breast
- Pinch sea salt
- 1 tsp Sesame oil
- 1/4 Cup Coconut flour
- 1/2 tsp Ground ginger
- 4 Egg whites
- 6 Tbsp Toasted sesame seeds
- Cooking spray of choice

For the dip: *

- 2 Tbsp Natural creamy almond butter
- 4 tsp Coconut aminos (or GF soy sauce)
- 1 tbsp water
- 2 tsp Rice vinegar
- 1 tsp Sriracha, or to taste
- 1/2 tsp Ground ginger
- 1/2 tsp Monkfruit (omit for whole30)

Directions:

1. Preheat you air fryer to 400 degrees for 10 minutes.
2. While the air fryer heats, cut the chicken into nuggets (about 1 inch pieces,) dry them off and place them in a bowl. Toss with salt and sesame oil until coated.
3. Place the coconut flour and ground ginger in a large Ziploc bag and shake to combine. Add the chicken and shake until coated.
4. Place the egg whites in a large bowl and add in the chicken nuggets, tossing until they are all well coated in the egg.
5. Place the sesame seeds in a large, Ziploc bag. Shake any excess egg off the chicken and add the nuggets into the bag, shake until well coated.
6. GENEROUSLY spray the mesh air fryer basket with cooking spray. Place the nuggets into the basket,* making sure to not crowd them or they won't get crispy. Spray with a touch of cooking spray.
7. Cook for 6 minutes. Flip each nugget and spray for cooking spray. Then, cook an additional 5-6 minutes until no longer pink inside, with a crispy outside.
8. While the nuggets cook, whisk all the sauce ingredients together in a medium bowl until smooth.
9. Serve the nuggets with the dip and DEVOUR!

Air Fryer Chicken Drumsticks

Servings: 8 | **Cook Time: 25 Mins** | **Prep Time: 5 Mins**

Ingredients:

- 8 - 12 chicken drumsticks
- Seasoning*
- Oil (optional)

Directions:

1. Preheat the air fryer to 200C for 5 minutes.
2. Optionally brush the drumsticks with some oil.
3. Season the chicken drumsticks with your favourite spices. You can just use salt if you prefer.
4. Add the drumsticks to the air fryer basket. You might need to use a trivet to fit them all in, or if you have a smaller air fryer, cook them in batches.
5. Cook for 22 - 25 minutes, turning halfway through.
6. Check the chicken is cooked all the way through - they should reach 75C internally, use a meat thermometer if possible.

Air Fryer Rotisserie Chicken

Servings: 4 | **Cook Time: 1 hour** | **Prep Time: 5 Mins**

Ingredients:

- 1 Whole Chicken cleaned and blotted dry
- 2 Tablespoons Ghee (or high quality Coconut Oil or Olive Oil)
- 1 tablespoon tog house seasoning

Directions:

1. Remove giblet packet from chicken and pat dry.
2. Rub Ghee/Oil all over chicken and season generously.
3. Place chicken, breast side down into Air Fryer basket.
4. Cook at 350 degrees for 30 minutes.
5. Flip chicken over and cook for 350 degrees for an additional 30 minutes, or until internal temperature reaches 165 degrees.
6. Let rest for 10 minutes and then serve.

Air Fryer Hunter's Chicken

Ingredients:

- 2 chicken breasts (1 chicken breast per person)
- 4 rashers of bacon (1 or 2 per chicken piece)
- 6 tbsp BBQ sauce
- 50g grated cheese (cheddar, mozzarella, gouda or parmesan)

Directions:

1. Place the chicken breasts in the air fryer basket at 190°C/375°F and set the timer for 10 minutes; if you have a small air fryer basket, you might only be able to fit two at a time. Turn the chicken at the 5-minute mark.
2. After 10 minutes of cooking time, using some tongs or a fork, remove the chicken breasts and wrap each one in one or two rashers of bacon. To keep the rashers in place, you can use a cocktail stick.
3. Return the bacon-wrapped chicken to the air fryer basket and cook for a further 10 minutes, again turning halfway.
4. At the end of the cooking time, open the air fryer basket and brush the bbq sauce equally over each chicken breast.
5. Sprinkle the grated cheese over the top of the BBQ sauce.
6. Air fry for a further 2 to 3 minutes or until the cheese has melted and the bbq sauce is hot.
7. Remove from the air fryer, and remove the cocktail sticks if you used them.
8. Check the chicken is cooked all the way through, either by cutting into one or using a meat thermometer.
9. Serve with your favourite side dish.

Air Fryer Chicken Nuggets

Servings: 4 **Cook Time: 8 Mins** **Prep Time: 10 Mins**

Ingredients:

- 3-4 boneless chicken breasts
- 2 eggs, beaten
- 100g breadcrumbs, (approx)
- Seasoning of your choice, eg; 1tsp smoked paprika,
  1tsp garlic granules, 1/2 tsp salt, 1/2 tsp pepper.

Directions:

1. Cut chicken breasts up into small chicken nugget-sized chunks.
2. Set up a chicken nugget breading station of three bowls. Add the beaten egg to one bowl, mix the seasoning with the breadcrumbs, add to a different bowl, and put the raw chicken pieces in another bowl.
3. Using kitchen tongs, dip the chicken in the beaten egg, then roll it in the seasoned breadcrumbs. Place in air fryer basket.
4. Repeat with each piece of chicken. Depending on the size of your air fryer, you may need to cook in 2 separate batches.
5. Cook at 200°C (390°F) for 8 to 10 minutes. Check the chicken nuggets are cooked through before serving.

Notes

Instead of eggs, you can dip the chicken in melted butter.

Air Fryer Chicken Kiev Balls

Servings: 2   Cook Time: X Mins   Prep Time: X Mins

Ingredients:

- 300 g chicken (breast or ground), (12oz)
- 3 cloves garlic, crushed
- 100 g breadcrumbs, (3/4 cup)
- 120 g butter, (1/2 cup)
- 2 fresh parsley sprigs
- 1 egg

Directions:

1. Mix together the butter, chopped parsley and crushed garlic. You can use a food processor to do this, just don't over process it or the butter will go too soft.
2. Divide the butter out into 12 (ish) equal sized balls. Pop them in the fridge (or freezer if you are short on time), to harden up.
3. If you are using whole chicken breasts instead of already minced/ground meat then you will need to also run this through a food processor, or high speed blender.
4. Once your garlic butter balls have hardened up a little, it's time to start wrapping your ground chicken around them. Take a little bit of chicken at a time and wrap some around each butter ball as a thin layer, around 1 to 1.5cm.
5. Beat the egg in a bowl, ready to dip your chicken balls in. Set up another bowl with your breadcrumbs in. You can use day old bread and pop it in a food processor to turn it into small crumbs, or as I often like to do, keep some store bought breadcrumbs in the cupboard. Season your breadcrumbs depending on your tastes (salt, pepper, perhaps a little paprika if you want some extra flavour).
6. For the next step (and final part of the preparation!) I use some kitchen tongs. It makes it easier to dip the balls and ensure they are evenly coated all over. Firstly dip the ball in the egg bowl, then roll it around in the bowl of breadcrumbs. Make sure the breadcrumbs are holding on tight or the air fryer might blow them off. If need be use your hand to press them in firmer.
7. I sprayed them with a little oil (using an oil sprayer) and then placed them in my air fryer basket. I cooked them for 10 minutes at 200C/390F). Check half way through and turn over.

Notes

Side note: some people like to include some flour to this part of the process - they feel it helps the breadcrumbs hold to the meat better. I personally prefer to omit it (I don't notice a difference). If you want to include flour just dip the balls in the flour before the egg.

Printed in Great Britain
by Amazon